THE GRATEFUL DEAD

THE GRATEFUL DEAD

Hank Harrison

A STAR BOOK
published by
W. H. ALLEN

A Star Book
Published in 1975
by W. H. Allen & Co. Ltd.
A division of Howard & Wyndham Ltd.
44, Hill Street, London W1X 8LB

Printed in Great Britain by
Richard Clay (The Chaucer Press), Ltd., Bungay, Suffolk

ISBN 0 352 30093 0

For
Hermes Trismegistus
and the
Sunshine Children

He would only make himself ridiculous by quoting poetry to them which they could not understand. They would think that he was airing his superior education. He would fail with them if he were to take up a wrong tone.

James Joyce
The Dead

CONTENTS

FOREWORD TO THE BRITISH EDITION

The Dead Book is not a rock and roll book, a fact which has disappointed more than a few readers in North America. Since its publication in 1970 I have realized that people have been conditioned to seek cult information from rock and roll books that tends to elevate the rock stars and depress the reader. The Grateful Dead simply do not believe in this.

The original intent of *The Grateful Dead* was to present information about the life styles of San Franciscan bohemians past and present, while still flattening the affect and heroic status of anyone who sets him or herself above the audience. The Dead for instance know, from long experience, that the performance is usually no bigger than the audience. It was also my original intent to show the unglamourous grit of bohemian life, the toil of the workingman and the sorrow and anguish which besets every creative soul rich or poor on this planet . . . In fact *The Grateful Dead* was mentioned as a subversive document by the pre-Watergate government, a fact I have managed to be proud of.

It is for these political reasons that I was prompted to disguise a number of names for the North American edition that are now undisguised in the British Edition. For instance, I felt it politically expediant to change the name of Augustus Owsley Stanley, the famous LSD Baron, to Merlin. This gave him a cloak of secrecy during the time he was facing charges in America. For other reasons I changed the name of Margo St James to Mikto St Johns, but now that Margo has publicly announced that she wishes to organize the American prostitutes I see no need to mask her identity.

The Grateful Dead attempts to trace the evolution of the San Francisco Bohemian lifestyle purveyed by the gamblers and gold miners of the 1850s to the peak of the Haight Ashbury experience and the death of Flower Power in the late 1960s. The book then shifts its ampitheater to Europe and concentrates on Glastonbury and the Dutch Modernist movement . . . the next volumn will cover the era since the end of the Haight Ashbury.

The Grateful Dead was, in its original conception, an illuminated black and white, computer designed, multimedia, manuscript, originally including a recorded disc and a built in 16mm home movie scenario. This film script motivates the book and adds continuity by using a fictionalized narrative in many voices. The 'on camera' narrative is conducted by many individuals and they are named as they appear, but the omniscient voice is that of ghosts such as Neal Cassady, or Lenny Bruce or Charlie 'Yardbird' Parker or Janice Joplin or some other well known master of the North American oral tradition.

Finally, I would like to acknowledge my commitment to the preservation of the Glastonbury traditions as does The Grateful Dead and many other West Coast families who owe a deep debt to the works of the R.I.L.K.O. organization, the writings of John Michell, Francis Yates, Margret Murray, Keith Critchlow, Bligh Bond, Guy Underwood, William Sterling, Kathryn Maltwood and John Watkins.

H. H. 1975

FOREWARNED

The Grateful Dead is a family, a large, amorphous patriarchy. It can be considered as large as all sentient souls or as small as an omega-minus particle.

The Grateful Dead is an esoteric secret brotherhood, fortuitously gathered, and an exoteric rock and roll band that plays loud music and sounds different at different times in front of vast audiences of 'wild, screaming, drug-crazed dropouts in their mid-twenties.'

The Grateful Dead is the Mula Dhara Chakra, the platinum wires that shoot energy to the cosmic brain, the cobra unfolding in the shadows, and the Aztec calendar biting its tail in the ever-expanding universe. By now everyone in the family has taken a vow to cease sufferings in the neighborhoods of the minds of the hells and heavens – and anywhere a talon can be inserted.

This, then, this gypsy aristocracy spitting back at the empire is the family, and they all remember what hell it was, what a fearful nightmare it was. What crawling out of a frozen garbage can is like, what really going mad is like. Not being able to remember how you got beat up or how Frank died or how Jack Schwadron went mad and ate his own hallucinating fingers behind poison mushrooms and remembering the dyke that cut off her tit and part of the time not caring.

They all remember the disgusting little nauseas seen on walks through thick fog, the stigmatic bleeding statue of St Francis, and you all high on acid, hoping to see its smile and finding out (what a crash it is to find out) . . . they moved it to Fisherman's Wharf because it had ruined the tableau of weddings and funerals and cracked the tilting marble steps of the Church of St Francis of Assisi.

They all remember a bunch of weird people, died and nearly died, and worse, lived through their youth with half a mind and a robot soul. Some can't read about themselves for fear of the daemons it may bring back, some are closet beatniks with a job downtown, carrying a sleeve of tears for the drunken blacks who had no rights ever and the guy who died of diabetic seizures because it looked close to drunkenness on the floor of the tank, flippin' and jerkin' and bashin' his head. And the cops not carin'.

Anyone who saw Ginsberg on TV and dropped out and played jazz and wore a beret and let his hair grow a little longer knows what it's all about. But anyone who stayed home and went to ballgames ten years ago couldn't have followed the Zen path: It's very narrow, it's mutually exclusive. There was only one door open in and around San Francisco, and a finite number of curiosity seekers took the opportunity to pass like the Elu of the Nine in Masonic ritual. An even smaller number found their way to Menlo Park in 1965, to a pizza parlor called Magoo's. Magoo's was just a place, prosaic and accidental, on a clean, upper-middle-class street. But Magoo's is where the Grateful Dead started. The San Francisco Sound. It was a small sound by present standards, but it started before LBJ or the moon landings.

People had gotten together and they all heard the sound for the first time and they could still hear it a week later, tingling on the lips. They felt it in the air, the sheer magnetic mantra. They knew it was apocryphal because they had never heard anything like it before. So it was a new human experience being had . . . there in Magoo's.

That was when the bubble jelled. To be ripped open and blown up again a thousand times. White magic and the antagonist – black magic lurking in some sinister corner. The impression stored in crystals of a sugar cube brought all the way from New York, from IFIF:

If what?
International Federation for Internal Freedom
The last time Tim Leary saw sanity.

There it was, this little montage of history inside this little sugar cube and it all happened simultaneously on a white pedestal on a purple pillow with the gold tassels – the crown jewel of all heads – the first LSD.

Internal Freedom but not external – music worked on externals. The music worked from the crust inward . . . the acid etched from the inside out . . . and the music progressed from pizza parlors to topless joints to the Acid Test to the college campus to the Philharmonic to wax grooves rotating at 33⅓ rpm to celluloid passing a shutter at 16 fps to GOD and, finally, to peace, we hope.

The serious sound of free music finally crept its way out to the ladies lost in the Wurlitzer in Hayward, South Chicago and Scarsdale. You can hear it in your icebox . . . Hear the socialism humming? That's the magic!!

Yes, you can be frightened of them! They are real and they have grown to be many and they are happy but deadly serious, armed to the teeth and extremely intelligent. They are as powerful as painted buses and battalions of tie-dyed, uniformed marijuana smokers, young and old. They are as powerful as a sunset at Big Sur, which sets twice – once for the clouds and once for the prophets who dot the cliffs and inhabit the seal rookeries . . .

Terrifying, huh? That's it, that's the magic!

That's where the plots are hatched to overthrow the kingdom, and it's inaccessible to the unwashed. Only the Zen Master knows the shibboleth.

The new music, you see, is the airborne detergent that broke down the walls.

It was Joshua's music. The lamb ram sheep horn shofa holy music. Transmuting molecules into wafers to be consumed as peyote buttons and holy eucharists.

Eerie musical notes, glowing, bringing up a generation to a sacred level of consciousness through mantra chanting, electronic pulsations, and, of course, random consultation with the *I-Ching* and the *Tarot*.

They are mad, not angry, just mad. Edgar Allan Poe-dying-in-the-gutter mad.

The music was all they had for awhile. The music was a sane sound in a psychotic universe. And the maddest of all was Neal Cassady.

Everybody presently involved in the Grateful Dead business must have followed Neal Cassady's path to and from the East Coast at least five times each between 1960 and '68. And they must have had their *Travels with Charley* and their *Air-Conditioned Nightmare* à la Henry Miller. Because it was traditional to do so, because they were the ultimate Hungarians, the final wave of savages let loose from the zoo ghetto deep suburbs of middle-class Amerika.

There wasn't no sense trying to stop them, parents plead as they might. 'Cause the mother magnet drug them, some somnambulistic, some running from Sacrament to Sacramento, and even on tippy-toe caution to the San Mateo Peninsula south of San Francisco where the free music finally got free, and the parts to this jigsaw power puzzle swung into place like doors in a Flash Gordon serial, teeth meshing as if they were somehow all being masticated by some relentless gargantuan mandible. On any day at Kepler's Book Store, near Stanford University, there'd be ten or twenty gimp pervert geniuses looking at each other and swimming around in this power soup. Knowing reality was all dumb, and simultaneously knowing it was them who were chosen to do something because San Francisco was on its usual bummer. So was New York. San Francisco had just produced the Kerouac and Ginsberg and Ferlinghetti phalanx and New York was pooped from the abstract expressionists.

NOW it was Music's turn. And they all knew that; at least, they knew it was doom time for the writers. The painters might as well lie out in the freeway. They knew the musicians were the oracles and the fonts of life for the time being, so they all grabbed on in a subconscious semi-automatic response to chaos and started banging, singing, moaning, plucking, strumming, plugging in. Anything that made music was OK. Anybody that made music was OK; the criticism didn't come until later. Everyone started doing music numbers, learning to play, sing or write. Those who had little or no performing skill gathered around as appreciative audiences. Hootenannies sprung up on almost any provocation. Teams formed, idols were worshiped, gurus were sought. Jazz with poetry, flamenco, bongos, beer bottles, weed; all the paraphernalia got found almost as if this new West Coast music thing was a zany incomplete treasure hunt that could never end until some unknown destiny was met, until all of the participants got what they needed, until all of the players learned to use the dissonant energies. It was a mini-max game . . . no one loses, everyone wins, and everybody gets high.

SAN MATEO

And from that skull distilleth
a dew upon him which is external
and filleth his head daily
and from that dew which floweth
down from his head
the dead are raised up
in the world to come.
– The Greater Holy Assembly

The first day of the spring semester, 1959, Gladstone Odduck stumbled into the College of San Mateo, on Coyote Point, and blew his mind, saved from an unfortunate suicide in the suburbs, in open shirt and in good enough shape to swim a 100-meter backstroke in almost a minute, sports coat and tennis shoes, a budding sumo wrestler.

On the first day he met all the energy centers. It was simple – they were all in one place over by the door at the first electric table, the place which seemed to glow. The Electric Table clique.

The eating complex at this little tree-studded college was rather uncomplicated. Giant barns, chicken coops, random landscape, head cook is gate cop's wife.

Overlaid on this dumb portable architecture was a bustle horde of students sort of going to school underneath a blanket of airport take-off kerosene, able to overlook the San Mateo yacht club while eating a bag lunch.

A full 70% of the student body were men; and of those, most were wounded or disabled in some way. Korean War vets with steel plates in their heads, shell-shocked guys, guys that froze and skinny guys that got captured. The archetypes were all there, except nobody came back from Korea strung out on smack! These guys all wore crew cuts, drank beer, always wanting to organize everything, start a fraternity and fuck 'broads.'

The other 29% of the campus population was super

squares, or what some kids used to call PADDY ASS: You know, DeMolay, Job's Daughters, all that storefront Masonic bullshit, but this kind of student body is what was expected of a community college in 1960, and the College of San Mateo had prestige.

San Mateo is the spine of the Bay Area. The communities of Hillsborough and Atherton are both within the boundaries of San Mateo, and these are the two richest-per-capita communities in the state. The San Francisco Airport is in San Mateo, the ballpark is almost in San Mateo, the majority of the City's commuters head south at night and even the San Francisco County Jail is in San Mateo. So this little college became a sparking place on the path of more than a few.

The Electric Table was the home base for the one percenters who were neither Paddy Ass nor Vets. Late bloomers sat at the Electric Table, jazz buffs, the constitutional psychopathic inferiors, borderline muftis and pill freaks. Doug Naughton had migraines and drove a real Cord automobile, Pat Britt stuffed his baritone sax with beers and waded into the ocean. That was the Electric Table. It became a clique out of self-preservation, since the Paddy Asses were actually getting threatened and telling the administration via parents that two niggers and a bunch of weirdos were actually getting 'A's' in college. But the majority, ruled by the Vets, didn't give a shit, and the school went about its usual psychic sleep, uninterested in the fears of the Paddy People.

In the midst of this sat the Troll, clad in a sport coat which looked like a San Quentin kick-out suit. Troll was Norwegian and only five feet high in his knickers. Six years later, after he takes acid, he finds himself with a long beard and a longing for Valhalla, but at the time, there in college, in 1960, nobody wanted to type anybody – all just greatly interested in accepting and being accepted.

This table is where the Jazz Band hung out. Dick Crest and Bud Young's Jazz Band. Odduck and Phil Lesh hit it off from the first day. There were insane jam sessions in the lounge. Odduck would go on five-day Wyamine runs and sit around and listen to the sessions and think about things.

To Odduck, Lesh, the trumpet player, seemed to be the most brilliant guy in the crowd: the craziest, too. He was aggressive and smug, yet compassionate. They used to call him the ALABASTER ÜBERMENSCH . . . but who ever heard of a skinny Übermensch?

One day, for diversion, Lesh, Odduck, Troll, Lenny Lasher, the bass player and Pat Britt, the baritone sax guy, decided to take some women up to the City and sit in with a Salvation Army band on the corner of Third and Howard, like a real skid row scene. Everybody thought it was too much to hear Phil play 'The Saints Come Marching In' two octaves above the signature. Grossed out the Salvation Army.

They were nineteen years old then. And they were all poor and took to stealing lunches and books to get through, but they stopped that because Troll stole his own lunch one day.

Odduck and Phil decided to get an apartment, and that's where lots of trouble started. Third Avenue in San Mateo was left over after the freeway went through, and on it were constructed some fresh new apartment houses, wedged between some old wood frame places and some almost-ghetto homes called Shoreview (which have sunk three inches a year, which means they are almost awash by now).

Just slap down some Bay mud and slam down a house. Nowadays the techniques are more profound: Dredgers go out farther and pollute the Bay more, but you notice it less because the designers build canals so that you can drive your boat up to your backyard barbecue pit and avoid the freeway, which is out to eight lanes and bumper to bumper. *IN SEISMOLOGY THERE EXISTS A PHENOMENON KNOWN AS LIQUEFACTION, WHICH MEANS BAY FILL TURNS TO QUICKSAND IN AN EARTHQUAKE!*

Well, back in 1960, Odduck and Phil moved into one of those fresh new places on a freeway bypass route. Nothing to do but sit around and bullshit a lot because they didn't have much dope then. None, in fact. So that's what they'd do: sit around and bullshit and eat.

Phil would stay up all night (many nights a week) and compose symphonies in the kitchen corner under a fluorescent light that hummed in B-flat, while Odduck stayed in the other corner by the bathroom and splashed paint on grandiose canvases, which have all disappeared now. The reason they stayed up all night was because they had the grave misfortune to be economically underprivileged at the time.

They had to take on a third roommate, Jim Cooke, whom they didn't like but who had a job and paid more than a third of the rent. While Cooke snored and dreamed of his next football conquest, Phil and Odduck stayed up and consulted the muse and sometimes stared out the window at the street through the blue rain.

Sometimes when they were bored they would sneak out and prowl around and put an oil slick on the road just at a braking point for a very sharp curve, and then retire to their second-story window to watch the spinouts. But it never happened; nobody ever spun out. They tried soap chips, oil, water and other combinations, but nobody ever fell for it except on one occasion about a month later when they hadn't even tried and it wasn't even raining.

A girl from the college missed the turn in a '58 DeSoto and crashed into the garage below, knocking out the brace which held up the front of the apartment, which was unpleasant as Odduck was composing poetry in the bathtub at the time. The bellowing horn and the girl's screams soon brought some sense about the matter as the neighbors gathered about in various stages of undress. Odduck envisioned himself a hood ornament spewing forth water in a sort of mannequin pis pose, and Phil to this day thinks his toilet flushing was so synchronous as to cause the girl's brakes to fail. After that they abandoned the oil slick idea for more constructive pastimes. And the girl wasn't hurt. Phil comforted her all that night.

When they were hungry enough to do desperate things, they'd rob the local grocery of food for the week. This was done in a rather simple manner, as they had no knowledge of the consequences, nor could they afford to care. Fate was on their side as this was all done before the police published statistics about crime waves and petty theft and increased losses to merchants, so that no stores had, as yet, installed mirrors and cameras and *This store is protected by* signs . . .

which measures are supposed to scare off prospective thieves.

They simply went shopping and filled the cart with the goods, added a few bottles of wine, and on one occasion vodka, and then, as if they belonged there, put everything in brown-paper produce bags and wheeled the cart out the back door. Of course, there was the dangerous section, crawling on hands and knees Iwo-Jima style to the highway and safety.

In addition to writing symphonies, Phil was composing atonal jazz compositions for the College of San Mateo Jazz Band, mostly in B-flat, and playing trumpet in the band and freaking out on his new oval mouthpiece. He never practiced at night but waited until everyone was gone in the morning. Then he would work up his chops and practice new runs with the freaky axe which, luckily, the neighbors dug. The farther away you got, the more it sounded like Maynard Ferguson screeching back at Cat Anderson, blowing back at Conni Condoli.

Phil's mind wasn't on the mouthpiece; it was on the sound, and his heart was in the symphony he was writing: SUN CYCLE. There were other symphonies, most of which were torn up and disposed of after many fluorescent nights of india-ink drafts on that expensive music paper he could get only in Berkeley. He tore them up because he felt he was plagiarizing from Stockhausen or Walter Piston. But he knows now there is no plagiarism – just synthesis – just divine revelation. No one person can possibly gather it all up. There are no more Bacons – no more Tychos – no more Plinys. Omniscience is for the very dim past and the very remote future, where man can finally listen to himself come in Stereo.

Odduck said:

In the days at Coyote Point, all dreams were incense dreams. A complete technology was out of the question. We didn't understand the pre-existing civilization, and we thought we would never see the day when the objective mind served the computers with proper ideas of ethics and compassion and fed all the absolute facts (there are only a few) into the data

banks and coupled the inner working to a realtime universe clock that read out the exact location of planets and their oppositions at all times and gave a visual feedback that was legible, so that the solar system could be sped up or retarded to any point in the future or any point in the past – accurately. Instant astrology? No, actually instant planetary influence correlations – that's what we were after. We knew nobody was going to build us gypsies a starship. We'd have to do it ourselves.

Now, at the same time, and unbeknownst to the Electric Table clique, a guitarist and gadfly named Jerome Garcia was attending sociology classes at C.S.M. and tripping out in night school, accompanied by his famous sidekick, Bob Hunter. Both were free spirits, and both were in no hurry to do anything.

Garcia had just managed to wiggle out of the Army's mind control and was sick of the hassle. In the Army, he was attached to a public relations unit which was set up to demonstrate and display the advantages of the NIKE-Hercules missile.

Here now, children. Here we have the nose cone, and here, underneath the ramp, we have the guidance control system . . .

Nobody blamed him for dropping out or for refusing to take the goddamn thing onto a school ground.

Still and all, Coyote Point was a heavy trip before the bay got polluted, before the Whole Earth, before JFK, before acid was even heard of, much less made illegal.

FLASH FORWARD TO SPRING 1972. GARCIA IS TALKING TO A REPORTER ON AN AIRPLANE, CIRCLING LIKE A CONDOR IN AN AERIAL STACK OVER GOTHAM CITY, U.S.A.

I know that there's no value to just showing one side of the picture. We have to illustrate what's there.

Summer of 1970 was just one diabolical bummer after another. Phil's father died of cancer, my mother died in an

automobile accident, one of the kids was killed on a bicycle – it was just like there was death happening, cascades of weird shit falling down around our ears. So there we were in the studio, creating this thing, pullin' together, and because we managed to get off under those circumstances the music has a certain quality.

Others died later – Weir's folks both within one month of each other. Johnnie Dee's baby 'Buddha' was caught in a fire. But there's a whole crop of babies being born.

It's a matter of being able to change with the time. Change is the nature of the universe, and the way people should be relating to it is just to flow. It seems to work, because despite how weird it's gotten – and it's gotten weird in every way at one time or another (we've been assaulted by every kind of bummer, we've had splits among ourselves) – it's still been a very slow, very gradual climb. I don't know where it's climbin' *to*, but . . .

Initially, when we started the Grateful Dead, we didn't have anything goin' anyway. We were nowhere, but it was groovy. That 'nowhere' state is a thing that everybody can revert to and be cool behind. So we're not losin' or gainin' anything, we're just goin' through the changes. And the changes have brought us this far, and showed us this much, and they're continuing to take us along. That's the ride we're on.

The only way I can describe it is that I consider this a very important time to be alive, and a big jackpot. Aside from that, everything is speculation. Who knows what's going on? In my version of the universe, it's far out, things are far out, there's more than meets the eye in every situation. Big things are happening on the globe, it's an important time, you dig?

If we blow it this time, there's not gonna be anyone left to blow it again. All the bummers of this era are coming to a head. All California, all America, has smog now. The death forces are all over. This is the time, man. It's either got to pull out of this, shape up and get together (even marginally would make it, even a close one would make it), or else . . . it could so easily go into complete oblivion, poison environment, fuck up the earth, end of life.

THERE IS A LONG PAUSE

For awhile we were entertaining the notion of finding a big piece of land in Canada, and living up there, taking our whole scene up there and forgetting about the United States. But then the flash came down about there's no place you can run to on the planet Earth. The SEA isn't clean . . . in the middle of the Pacific there's styrofoam cups and plastic Japanese fishing floats. There's no getting rid of that stuff, because nothing eats it.

So, realistically, there's nowhere on the planet to go, except maybe to buy yourself a little time. But time for what? Time to die a little slower? It's not so much you and me and cigarette butts and beer cans – that's just little shit. It's the big-time industrial shit that's doin' it, causing the really devastating poison.

The best new development is that there's a lot of good people, good minds and good heads, who are into media with the traditional sense of responsibility, but without the traditional bullshit. So there's a possibility, finally, for people. It's sort of the same position we're trying to wheedle for ourselves in the music industry – so there's as little between us and getting it on as there can be. We're already well into what we've got. And it's more than we ever expected any of us to have – access to beautiful tools.

THE PLANE IS IN GLIDE PATH NOW.

Technology is a giant toy maker and we should trip out behind it. Whenever there are times of stress, entertainment trips go way up. People need it; you gotta have something to get high with. I can envision a time when everybody has a television set with a yes/no switch on it. And whenever anything of any importance comes up, the computers do a printout of the facts and information on all sides of any question, and everybody instantaneously votes. Immediately, everything is reprogrammed to take that into consideration, and the whole galaxy seems to work beautifully (sometimes).

CUT TO HELICOPTER SHOT OF COLLEGE CAMPUS.

Coyote Point was named by Spanish settlers and visited by their Franciscan monks. It had been designated by the earth god as a raw jut above the serene backwash of the Bay, which was how the Indians enjoyed it. The monks planted the unique gum tree *eucalyptus*, the tree of the Holy Eucharist. The tree sacred to the Indians, who were beaten by the Spanish, who were pushed out by the gringos wild with gold-fever. So it goes . . . no honor among thieves. With the outrage of the airport, all the coyotes left. San Mateo College was a school for scoundrels. A place where sparks flew. It was the maelstrom of the aforementioned magnet. Everyone fell by and said WOW! this is the farthest out thing yet . . . ya can freak freely and no one cares.

Slamming into San Mateo after living in Sonoma or Ukiah – any of those California cow towns – was an immediate cosmic experience akin to the Cossack child being loosed from his swaddling. Like, if you want a true Damascus experience, spend eighteen years in abject mediocrity and then one day leave it all as sudden, as fast as possible . . . as you cross the bridge you can see this neon sign: Big Daddy Nord, dressed up like Uncle Sam, points at you and screams at the top of his bronchospasmic lungs . . .

UNCLE FREAK NEEDS YOU, DADDY-O!!!

So they joined up, six or seven hundred, from all around. They joined God's little freak army with no destination or purpose that they could guess at and maybe they were too gone to guess.

About 1959 or so, Phil met Mike Lamb, who was the first direct connection to Palo Alto. Now this Lamb fellow was a bright, tall, bond Mensa reject. He had all the brains but dug chasin' the ladies too much. More aware than Phil or Odduck, and he was linked up somehow to Perry Lane, Ken Kesey and the crowd. Lamb felt lazy a lot; rich kid anyway. Mother studied Japanese brushpainting, and

Dad – never dropped around the pad except to sleep and catch a bit of toast for breakfast. Sister was a debutante.

Frankly, for all his intelligence; Lamb did very little. Later he had his monkey in Berkeley and worked at the Renaissance Coffee House in '62 on the corner of Shattuck and Channing Way. When things finally got rolling he started a group called Edsel Boogie, an incredibly apt name – half obsolete and 4/4 time. The group lasted four years or so and later became Freedom Highway, which is struggling to be remembered. Just one of the groups that proliferated anonymously in San Francisco from '65 to '69 and forever. Like the Mystery Trend out of Art Institute, or The Sparrow, which later became Steppenwolf out of Berkeley.

Lamb connects up a lot of things . . . sensed the tension in the air and bought a rust-blue Jawa Jupiter which was parked outside Kepler's. He invited a lot of people to those parties at Perry Lane.

Anonymous diary note: Spring 1960:

> **the party last week was such a freak show . . . intriguing – the girl who itched her tracks and warmed her arms up over the stove. Kesey and a hoard of the Khan's campfollowers arrived and just as quickly left who knows why, maybe because they had another mysterious gesture to articulate somewhere off at Half Moon Bay or out in God's notch somehwere.**

This was the protophase of the Pranksters. Kesey was working under his Ford Foundation grant. Everyone was impressed, but something about a cuckoo nest. Weird. He'll never get that published. Too cryptic!! He moved on to some other dirty palace of bucolic truth. Trying to tell everyone that maybe the hicks had some kind of a nit-pickin' crystal ball.

Finally, Phil and Odduck disbanded the place on Third Avenue, mainly due to an overcrowded condition: people sleeping in hammocks and in the bathroom, and Pat Britt, the saxophone man, getting stuck in the attic and beating the icebox through the wall. Ralph Del Carlo moved in and fucked everything up with his conga drums and his wine bottle on the respectable front wall, which he called The Poop Deck in moments of lesser sobriety.

Anyway, everybody had to leave and the summertime came. Odduck went to jail for stealing books, and Troll went off to hang some more paper and try to straighten things out in Sacramento.

After jail in Oakland and Santa Rita Rehabilitation Center, appropriately titled 'Greystone,' Odduck repaired to San Mateo one more semester and finally moved to San Jose and got married. Phil went to Napa to live with his folks for awhile and work in a bank, then came back to San Mateo to get enough credits to get into Cal-Berkeley, but he didn't see Odduck; instead, he fell in with the Troll.

In the autumn of 1961, the Troll and Phil lived together on Catalpa Street (Catalpa means *Head with Wings*). Phil started going down to Palo Alto with Mike Lamb more often, and it so happens that some guns were stolen from some place and the police came. They never found the guns. The Troll was so convincing, the police never bothered to search under his bed, from which, after the heat split, he produced two Mauser-actioned hunting rifles and an antique Zouave.

More than anyone else, the Troll was always running the risk of jail, a desperado in the midst, a symbol to all who knew him that they, too, were outside the culture, outside the established pattern. And not caring; in fact, less each day.

On one of these days, with nothin' better ta do, Phil and Lamb went off to Perry Lane to check things out and to hang around. Nobody home, so they went inside and sat down and drank a little wine. But over in the corner was Kesey's office, and Mike couldn't resist the temptation to sneak in and look around. He found the manuscript Kesey was working on: The Cuckoo's Nest Document. Ridiculous title, but a chance to read it. Lamb said: 'Hey, this is very good.' His face lit up. 'Very good.' Lamb wouldn't be Kesey's last critic. Phil took Mike's word for things and they split with a secret to think about. The bastion had been breached. Kesey was real – at least in those days he was real.

Anyway, Perry Lane was a tree-lined, rutty road, and there was some marijuana around, but mostly vin rosé and Bali-Hai and clunky cars, earmarked for doom. Stanford Shopping Center went right in and covered up even the ghosts. Ah, yes, good old plastic Menlo Park. More of the mediocrity that made LSD such a clever idea.

A swaggering hipster named Laird hung around Perry Lane a good deal and thence also came Jerry Garcia and others of no name and others forgotten. There was a girl standing in the dust at the doorway at one of the places up on Homer Lane, pregnant like out of Tobacco Road but not caring; not sad, just not caring. This was the Oregon genre, the Kesoid stuff, down-home baked beans and wilderness, a complete urban anachronism.

CUT TO SPRING 1971. ART NOUVEAU LIVING ROOM.

Harrison: In writing my book I've had trouble expressing the consciousness of the contemporary music. I certainly don't want to use that well-worn and inept acid-rock, folk-rock cliché. I want to distinguish contemporary music from show biz. 'There was a huge value difference between the concept of show biz and the concept of music, unrecorded music as played in San Francisco in the early days. The Trips Festival was music and it was "serious" music.' But that's a cliché, too.

Phil: But it was music that was seriously intended to get you high. It wasn't serious in the sense of deadpan. In a sense it was both high farce, just like the Acid Tests, and it was music that actually changed people's personalities. It was warping. There we were all together. Somehow the music would make us act in unison, but it was only one of the factors in that impulse. True, it was the loudest individual factor (aside from LSD). But only because you've really got to have something to relate to, especially when reality is hitting you right in the guts.

H: It was pure music in those days. It was innocent. There was something for everyone within that nucleus of music. I don't

mean 'Big Brother.' That's another concept. I don't mean 'The Charlatans' or any other group around. I mean that the Grateful Dead specifically had a cerebral level, a rhythmic level, and a very funky Pig Pen level, with other levels all mixed in together so that there was something for everyone.

P: There is also an Owsley level and a Kesey level that still haunt us occasionally. But electricity is what really does it. It's the Gutenberg Galaxy in the sense that electricity conveys the musical meaning as heavy as the music itself. Even now, rock records are starting to sound refined. Not only that, but the refinements are starting to sound musical. In other words, more global. All the toys of the technology are just starting to mature.

H: Were the Beatles aware of the electronic technology at any point?

P: I think so. I thought so from the beginning. Take 'Strawberry Fields' and 'I Am the Walrus.' Their style and techniques got more sophisticated and it started sounding better and better. Maybe it was George Martin more than anything else? Or maybe they intuitively understood 'AM Car Radio' stations mixing/combining/alternating to fit into Joe Mustang's concept of music.

H: What about the Rolling Stones?

P: Well, the Stones were into the *sound* of their music, I think, more than the Beatles were; they still are. And their music, too, has got more sophisticated; much more texture than there was before. They haven't gone in the same direction as the Beatles. The Beatles went in a more conventional direction. Into conventional kind of voice leadings and that sort of thing. The Stones are into lapidary kinds of music – in other words, layers of music. But their music smells funny – a bit too commercial for me.

H: You're on one of the David Crosby albums, and I noticed David gave you a Martin (d-24) for your very own. The tone

of this $1200 Martin is unbelievable. So to me there are layers of music just within that one guitar that don't exist on other 'good' guitars. Now from the first strum, the tone of that Martin gave you a flash . . . I saw your eyes light up. Did you have this same experience with your first instruments?

P: Yes, I started out with a stringed instrument, the violin. It was the highest thing I could find. It always got me high, but I never learned to play very well. I was eight years old when I started playing the violin. I played it about six years and then gave it up for the trumpet.

H: That's a fantastic contrast in instruments. Was the trumpet more of an adolescent trip?

P: Right; most definitely. So I played the trumpet until I was about twenty and then I quit.

H: You played trumpet on 'Born Cross-Eyed.' Just a little riff. I dug it; wish there had been more. But playing trumpet with a band is considerably different than composing. Where did you make the transition from playing to writing?

P: That is very subtle. It was part of the adolescent trip. It was part of the trip that led me to play trumpet. I just wanted to do more. Playing second violin was not enough. It was a pretty empty scene. I thought playing trumpet was 'it.' What I learned from the guy who taught me trumpet was a whole lot about musicianship in general.

H: Who was that?

P: A guy named Bob Hanson. He taught in Berkeley – still does. His sons have come to see us at the gigs. Bob has three kids, and they were learning to play all the instruments they could. I'd have loved to have been one of those kids. He was kind of a father to me at the time. A real hail-fellow-well-met kind of guy. We would spend most of the time rapping and joking. My mother would bitch because we had more goof-offs than trumpet lessons, but I learned to be a professional from that guy.

H: Was your mother at the lessons sometimes?

P: Well, we had a pretty small house.

H: Oh, he'd come over to your house.

P: Yeah, he'd come by on his route. He was just a good old guy, a real good musician, and he got me so I could play in orchestras with him. There I was, playing trumpet instead of violin, which is considerably more of an exposed and responsible place. Playing bosser music with adults and professionals instead of violin in kid orchestras. Somehow, I could pick up the trumpet fast enough so that in two years I was playing symphonies, whereas before it took six years to play the violin and I couldn't get far enough to play really well. Through all that, I got into an appreciation of musicianship which struck the long-forgotten chord which led me into music in the first place . . .

H. What was that?

P: I got this huge hit from the Brahms Symphony when I was four years old.

H: The first recollection of music was the Brahms Symphony?

P. Brahms First Symphony, conducted by Bruno Walter and the New York Philharmonic sometime in 1944. I heard it on the radio. My grandmother said, 'Philip, come listen to the nice music on the radio.' I walked over and sat down next to my grandmother (who I dearly loved – anything to be next to my grandmother). And wooow! This fucking thing comes out of the radio and knocks my head off. I have never been the same since. But dig this irony: Six years later, when I was ten, my violin teacher took me to hear the same conductor performing the same symphony in San Francisco. It was a big evening for me; I got to go out to dinner with my violin teacher. Very reinforcing.

H: When did you start to write jazz compositions?

P: About 1956 or so. Jazz was where it was at. The reason I switched high schools was because I could get harmony lessons elsewhere. They wouldn't teach me anything about what I really wanted to know. You see, I spent the first two years at marching band at El Cerrito. It was marching band and social studies time. They didn't have any harmony classes at El Cerrito and no ear training classes. They didn't have any kind of classes except fucking blowing your horn on the band master's chart. So I went to Berkeley. It was really a good flash for me because I was the new kid at school and one thing I could do was play trumpet. Another reason I left the school was I could play trumpet as good as the guy in the first chair, but the band master wouldn't let me play and all the other bullshit. He thought it would be bad for my head, but all it did was put me very uptight.

H: So you became Wagnerian for awhile?

P: True. Sad but true!

H: Didn't the same thing happen at San Mateo in the jazz band with Buddy Powers and Dick Crest?

P: Yes, but Buddy had all the wind and the chops to get all the really high stuff which that chair, in that band, really demanded. You had to have the endurance to stay up there all day, which I couldn't do. But he moved on, so I got the chair anyway. Al Molino was in that band, too. Some of the nerviest guys I ever met – Pat Britt, Lenny Lasher.

H: I remember you wrote two very pretty atonal charts in those days.

P: Actually, there were three, but the first never got through rehearsal. The other two I wrote were played at the concerts.

H: The very first one that was in rehearsal . . . what was that?

P: I don't remember. Something I wrote the first year I was there. It was awful hard. The acoustic bass player had to tune down his bass for the first line and then he had to tune it back up again for the whole rest of it. All the brass players started out in the highest register of their instruments and each section of the band was a different key. It was like blocks of granite sliding together. It was pretty weird for junior college.

H: Yeah, but it was a very advanced junior college. Did you know that Garcia and Hunter went to that same San Mateo Junior College at the same time, and also Rod Albin?

P: No I didn't. But a lot of weird people went there. So Garcia probably would have.

H: At that point it seems to me the music became secondary for the first time in your life. Trips started to be important. The good times.

P: Well, that came later on. After I had gone through the whole composition number. The experience of playing in big bands and writing compositions for big bands was one turning point. After that I was no longer interested in playing trumpet. I was interested in composing. I wasn't interested in playing instruments any more in a band where I was a part. I was interested in playing the whole band. From there it got heavier and heavier. At that same time I was into Ives and all that.

H. Also into all kinds of music – atonal jazz, Bartok, all-night sessions, Coltrane, Miles . . . remember?

P: At that time I was just raking it all in. That's the time when you're supposed to be learning. I had never known there was so much music, and all of it hung together so neatly.

H: At that same time you had a job in the college library, right?

P: That's right. My job was to judge the quality of incoming recordings. In other words, if they were scratched, I would send them back for duplicates. So I got to listen to all the new recordings. All the jazz and all the classical recordings.

H: Two years later you worked at KPFA for Gert Chiarito, 'Midnight Special,' as an engineer.

P: It was the same trip. You go where the information is, no matter what you have to endure or sacrifice. Luciano Berio was at Mills College at the time (1962). I had met Tom Constantin at Cal so we did our self-education number, since 'formal' school was actually retarded. I got away from Berio and composed the thing that was in me for that level. Then I didn't have anything more to say. That was in 1964. I wasn't doing anything for a while. Except getting high a lot.

H: What were you doing in the Haight besides delivering mail and fitting Jackson Pollock puzzles together? Weren't you composing anything?

P: Yeah, I was trying to compose some stuff. But that was about the time I got dried out. I came to the end of the road, and the opportunities for having what I had written performed were so limited, and the way I would have to channel my musical thinking was unpleasant to contemplate.

H: You had the Mime Troupe for small compositions.

P: Right, but those small compositions didn't get me off. The thing I had written in 1963 was a huge orchestral work called 'Foci' for four orchestras. It required 123 players and four conductors. Needless to say, it will be difficult to perform it.

H: What is your visual imagery like when you're performing live before an audience?

P: Since I first began seeing music I saw music as notes on spaces, sometimes colored, paisley, sometimes fragmented, and sometimes whirling notes and treble clefs with little feet running around them, but I see the notes we're playing all the time, at least the notes I'm playing as they are played. Sometimes the register is horizontal; sometimes waving like a flag. It seems like funny little cartoons sometimes, but I never see tangible seascapes or mountain sequences or pastoral roll-by or anything like that. I rarely have dreams of that kind either; they are almost always symbolic. It would be easier to define how high I am, what level of consciousness I'm at at any given time. If we've been on the road for thirty days we're usually very tired. It is always a thrill to play music live; that's what keeps us going with a smile. But what pisses me off is the crowd's screaming for more like at the Roman Circus after we've laid the finest riff out there already. That New York crowd screams for an encore no matter what; then go berserk if we don't take requests. That kinda fucks up the imagery.

H: What about when you hear a tape back during mix-down?

P: In that case, I have time to associate things to thousands of other things. I can feed it back on infinite loops in the studio, but that's where it gets weird because that's where the powers of criticism come to play; that's where the toys get really complex. So I'm free, but limited by the very thing that frees me. In that case the imagery is notes, symbols, and layers of music, plus anything else – classical forms, v.u. meter readings, etc. It's much more intense during a performance, and the studio is usually informal except when we're working against a deadline.

H: How does your classical influence come into the Grateful Dead music?

P: It hardly comes in at all. Only indirectly. Only in certain kinds of instances.

H: Is this the same with the jazz idiom?

P: I would say so. We've always tried to make the music as natural as possible in the sense that I, for instance, don't try to bring any kind of classical 'tricks' into the Grateful Dead.

H: But vast classical and jazz informations are stored in your educational computer.

P: Oh, yeah. All the data is there, and I draw on it subconsciously all the time, no doubt.

H: Just like Garcia touches on bluegrass and . . . whatever else.

P: True. But it's all very subliminal at this time. It's all like melted together into non-categories of stuff. I mean like there aren't any direct Beethoven influences or that sort of thing.

H: I was thinking more of things like Bartok and the atonal percussive pieces.

P: Well, I don't consider that truly classical music. That's sort of the precursor of what we're doing. It's like classical music is one extreme and what Bartok did is another, and we're the synthesis of those two extremes.

H: So, everything that happened in the 19th century was contra-Wagner. The Mahlers and the Stravinskys and so forth created a new energy force.

P: The four I consider to be the real creators of MODERN music are Ives, Debussy, Schoenberg and Mahler. Metaphysically they all sound very much alike.

H: When you say 'alike' you confuse me, because I perceive great, vast and subtle differences among those composers.

P: I mean, to the casual listener who's talking to someone while he's listening, it all sounds alike. This is how the majority of music gets listened to. If people would listen carefully the gimmicks would die out. But people habitually categorize music into simple, harmonic textures and dismiss it at that. Ives and Scriabin were using a pantonality context which involves the extremes of noise and dissonance and the extremes of consonance. That was their spectrum. Now the four composers I mentioned were able to make a synthesis somewhere on that transitional line between the two kinds of thinking. That's why they are valuable to me. I see them as precursors to what we are doing. In other words, we are attempting to create a music which involves the highest possible number of ways of playing all other music which has evolved in the world, even in the distant past, up to and including us. Those four guys together represent a plateau or hub or musical consciousness. Each of them was modern, but ancient at the same time. They were transcendental because they had resolved the time contradiction.

H: And you, with a five-man crew, have only been able to skim the very beginning of the surface?

P: That's absolutely correct, but it is only limited by our own inadequacies in our minds as to what we can do with our instruments; that is, of course, the instruments we are playing. Now consider Garcia – all of the shit he gets out of an electric guitar. They say that an electric guitar is a very limited instrument.

H: But he hasn't reached the bottom on that yet.

P: No, he certainly hasn't.

H: When he got into pedal steel that seemed to feed back to the electric guitar which fed back to the banjo, and that opened up new avenues. So, the guitar is only as limited as the cerebral cortex and the neural connections to the fingers. Garcia makes it look easy.

P: Yes, but I can't emphasize the word ELECTRIC enough. When I first played an electric instrument, I played it for seven hours straight, and I couldn't sleep that night. It got me so high that I knew something had to be happening. Something extremely different from acoustic. Then, of course, you start taking acid, and the phenomenon magnifies further, and you are hooked on ELECTRICITY. You start working with actual electronics and the amplifier without worrying about knobs or gauges. When we are playing I very rarely change anything but the knobs on my guitar. A slight volume change or switch between two distributions of sound. The rest of it is done with my hands. How I hit the string, how long I hold it, etc.!

H: The next logical thing would be to talk about your new electric bass. It seems to me that that instrument is a conceptualization which evolved from your early dreams of music unlimited. A way of opening up more business, more possibilities?

P: Yes, but always with the basis of the struck string and its overtones. It is infinite because the higher you go the closer they get together, so eventually they become noise. In the sound of the struck string there exists a microcosm of the entire spectrum of possibilities. When it's amplified, you can hear it all. That's what the electronics do – they amplify the overtones to a degree never thought possible in an acoustic instrument.

H: What about the giant Bach organs?

P: The overtones are mechanically limited and constructed and fed together like an electronic music machine. Like a Moog. Fed in together so you have your 16 foot stops with the pedal, and for each one of those 16 stops you have an 8-foot, a 4-foot, and a 2-foot, which are octaves of one another. So, depending on how the stops are arranged, any one or all five of those will sound when you hit one note on the pedal. With the struck string, they are all there; you only have to select or emphasize one with your finger or electronically with a foot pedal or a computer! With the organ, your control is limited.

H: So the new bass is quadriphonic, which will allow an array

of effects across the stage out to the audience. And you can stagger these effects as you see fit?

P: Yes, I have a six-position switch which Ron Wickersham has designed. This switch has the percussive distributions that I want.

H: It is true that with this amount of control you can actually create standing illusions – throw your voice, as it were?

P: Hopefully. It is going to depend a lot on the response of the system because bass notes seem to come from everywhere. That is the nature of bass notes; i.e., notes below 250 cycles.

H: Could that be because bass notes have always been played through monaural systems? They have never been played quadriphonically before in the history of music. So, this is going to be an exciting thing, to find out if you can localize those bass notes?

P: In a small room it definitely works. But the quadriphonic aspect is only half the trip of that bass. The other half is the regular system whereby the individual pickups, bass and treble, have a kind of tone control which gives you more flexibility. Most tone controls are simply a treble cut; they're really hard to get going. It is very hard to find the right setting. You have to keep experimenting endlessly.

H: This new bass also has a second stage which is still under development, is that right?

P: Actually, one is the bass and the other is the little black box with the pedal controls, which has some extra toys in it. The bass also has regular pickups with modern, efficient tone controls that actually boost certain frequencies and in certain band widths. Then it has the quadriphonic or the individual string pickup option. This, then, approaches a bass synthesizer concept. The foot-pedal black box would have four channels. It would essentially be the same thing as all of my four Fender pre-amps. It would have four inputs, and it would distribute itself to the four inputs in which I would have volume, treble and bass controls and a bright switch for each channel – which means 1400 watts of MacIntosh tube power. Yowee! In other words, I can control each speaker with those four channels plus a vibrato which would have a speed control and an intensity control. That would make the music sound fuzzed and go anywhere from a woooowoooowoooo to a rhhhhrhhhhrhhh. It would also have peak expander which expands the dynamics for 'precise' control of all four channels.

H: What is stage three?

P: This is the one that has to have the relays built into the neck.

H: Oh . . . the computer!

P: Yes. The blackbox servo will ultimately feed to an analog computer which will feed to a digital computer which knows what note it has to sound when a given fret is pressed. It scans the note and, depending on how hard I press, it stops. If I press very hard, it will go fast to the top of what it can see or perceive from the string and stop there. If I press a little softer, it will go up slower. It will be a complete and ultimately controllable thing. When I kick that in, I will be able to scan the note and bring out any harmonic I need – all with my fingers. It will also play conventionally. I won't have to play with any knobs. All with my left hand on the strings. That is the goal.

H: Total efficiency of movement.

P: Exactly. The only control on that bass, hopefully, would be a master volume and a function switch which will indicate pickups, quadriphonic, or computer, or whatever. Of course, the individual pickups would have volume controls on them for balance, but there would be very few tone controls.

H: Can you conceptualize writing music for that?

P: No! See, writing music has come to mean a whole different thing. THIS INSTRUMENT IS STILL AN ELECTRIC BASS. Even though it has more range than any bass instrument has ever had, it is still fundamentally a bass for use in a rock and roll band. Whereas if I wanted to get anything else out of it, I would have to start building in other tones like higher strings, or work with computers and octave-doublers. So then I could kick in an octave and I would get the note I was playing an octave higher. That would mean I would have to develop my technique to play bass lines down at the bottom and rhythm stuff in the middle, etc.

H: That's what I thought the treble cut was for . . . so you could play rhythm.

P: That is sort of what I'm after. Also, play bass and lead at the same time, in order to bring a more polyphonic concept into our band.

H: Wow! Zen consciousness!

P: Almost. That is what the big 'lady' has taught me. I call it a lady, you see . . .

H: Well, what has it taught you?

P: That all and everything is possible.

PALO ALTO

As we traveled Northward from the Table 0 degrees Capricornus maintaining a balance between atropine and muscarine, toward the mushroomical Taolands, a great light shone in the basement of the Peace Center there on the San Francisco Peninsula: the heavens opened and three squad cars busted the party, yes, halleluiah!

– Willy the Gate
Fragment from unfinished novel

If San Mateo was the incubator for the little Grateful Dead family movement, then Palo Alto was the first stage of external growth. Contrasted to the huge University of California at Berkeley, its arch rival, the Leland Stanford, Jr., Farm was isolated – usually warm and sunny, dotted with date palms and designed to resemble early California architecture. But the university population was dependent on the town of Palo Alto for after-hours kicks and any kind of nighttime culture; obversely, the town of Palo Alto was dependent on the campus for economic security. This is no longer the entire picture; Stanford has grown and industry has cropped up. But in the late 1950s, Palo Alto was simply 'that rich people's place down the Peninsula.'

In this milieu, poor met rich, there was some chance for some upward mobility, beer gardens and pizza parlors and bistros sprung up and the people who eventually formed the Grateful Dead community found life slightly more rewarding.

In February 1959, Willy the Gate was attending Redlands College, near Pomona. Somehow he got some Sandoz LSD from New York and took 50 mics., put colored lights in his dormitory room and listened to Bach with the other theology students. By 1960, Willy had flunked out of Redlands. He moved up to Palo Alto, saw the arches of St Michael's Alley and snapped that it was a good scene. This was the summer of Ken Kesey's first parties at Perry Lane, with everybody sort of filtering through the Peace Center, a place something like the Carmel Valley group around Joan Baez and Ira Sandoyster.

The political lines were clear – soft socialist, non-violent anti-fascist Trotskyite – but there was hardly any semblance of organization. There was the HUAC demonstration in 1960, when Mayor Christopher had the hoses turned on the peace and anti-bomb demonstrators. The first real head-bustin' most of us had seen. But more of that later.

Hostile? A bit. There were the catamarans *Everyman* and *Golden Rule* that went to sea to block nuclear testing in the Pacific.

Nothin' to do but hang out in Palo Alto, drinking coffee and letting the anxiety of how to stay alive keep your mind popping. Listen to Lord Buckley at Outside the Inside. Kenneth Rexroth read poetry at the Peace Center, which was now together enough to house people; Willy had a room inside, and like a good Christian, he put up various people too lame or stoned to find their way home.

A benefit was held for Kenneth Patchen, because Patchen actually had to pay income tax one year – made too much money and had to get up $600 to pay the govern god, sacrificial wampum. Patchen told everybody to stop making so much money and read his titles aloud:

An Astonished Eye Looks Out of the Air
A Surprise for the Bagpipe-Player
Before the Brave
Cloth of the Tempest
Fables & Other Little Tales
First Will & Testament
Glory Never Guesses
Hurray for Anything
Memoirs of a Shy Pornographer
Orchards, Thrones & Caravans
Panels for the Walls of Heaven

Pictures of Life and of Death
Poemscapes
Red Wine & Yellow Hair
See You in the Morning
Sleepers Awake
The Dark Kingdom
The Famous Boating Party
The Journal of Albion Moonlight
The Teeth of the Lion
They Keep Riding Down All the Time
To Say If You Love Someone
When We Were Here Together

He was over fifty then, but they all sort of dug him as autistic children might respect an older professional schizophrenic met in the hallways of an asylum.

The Patchen Benefit and other central happenings were held at Saint Michael's Alley, a place operated by a hip, middle-aged guy named Vernon Gates. St Mike's was a Spanish-facade coffee house on University Avenue, which was a nexus of activity, like Kepler's Book Store and the Tangent.

Five people would sit around a table and drink coffee. Then somebody would come in and lay something dark and sinister on the table, and then suddenly, as slowly as possible, but elated, the little clique would scuffle out to the street. Ten minutes later the same contingent would sidle back in, this time wearing dark glasses and symbolically announcing to the others that they had gone out to get high. That's how furtive everything was in those days. Now, everybody fires up grass in the streets, at theaters, at concerts, but it was very uncool to do that in those days. Maybe it still is.

FADE. CUT TO INTERIOR OF GRAY VICTORIAN HOUSE ON LITTON STREET.

What's all this sittin' around for? I can't just do this!

Garcia fixes guitars at Dana Morgan's, teaches guitar, too, but wants to be a painter, like Paul Speegle, but his paintings are lousy. He's had his head on guitars since the age of ten. The pressure was building. Garcia was done with AWOL Army, Presidio Army, Ford Ord, and looking for a little bread. Everybody would hang out at Kepler's like it was some anteroom for souls dying of ennui; and it was for years, providing croissants and coffee which nobody ever paid for hardly at all. Yah' see, many bookstores were distribution points for paperback versions of the hard-to-get hardbacks, which were too hard to steal 'cause they wouldn't bend. They chafed your belly and made a noticeable bulge in your pants which wasn't, but appeared to be, an erection.

FADE. LAP – DISSOLVE TO SHOT OF OLD HILLSIDE HOUSE NARRATOR # THREE:

There it was in the moonlight, run-down but roomy. Frank Serratoni's 'Chateau' in all its macabre destiny. The parties started, and Bob Hunter took some speed and wrote all day, and Willy the Gate and John Winter devised some astral plans in the courtyard. Danny Barnett ate his cornflakes and played drums, and Joe Novakovich started to get drunk. Garcia? Well, he found a place to practice.

1962 rolls around and there is the Chateau, all dusty and white, with the weeds around it, up on the hill. Chad and Sue invited Phil over to their place for a party. So along comes Tom Constantin and the spearmint wrappers. First, out into the kitchen for a beer and smackdabwhap in the middle of the kitchen sits Garcia – playin' and singin'. So Phil runs out to the lugubrious '56 Olds and fires its mufflerless engine up and he and Garcia cruise over to Berkeley to get T.C.'s lugubrious Webcor so's to make a kitchen tape. Kitchens have good acoustics.

DEEP, COLD, SPRING RAINSTORM, BAYSHORE FREEWAY, POINTING NORTH – ANOTHER SHORT INTREPID TRIP.

'Better fire this "J" up 'fore we get to the toll plaza' Treasure Island tunnel, just being built for up-and-down traffic, so there's a big huge bump in the middle of the bridge for awhile. Oldsmobile burps over the thing and down the under side of the bridge, which used to be the Key System A Train and trucks only and shoots over to Berkeley.

Garcia and Phil get to be great friends this night, with only one windshield viper working, they plotted the crashing cosmic view of the moment. Actually, Phil had it planned to get Garcia's tape played on KPFA, the 'subscriber-owned radio station' and local broadcast cell, which for the time being was the radio of Berkeley propaganda. Phil being the freebee engineer and ersatz program coordinator for Gert Chiarito, who had a late night hootenanny show called 'Midnight Special.'

Phil got the Webcor, took it back to Palo Alto that same night, recorded Garcia and played the tape the next day for Gert, who raved over it, and next thing ya' know, Garcia is playin' live on the radio . . . this radio being aired all over the Bay Area.

By 1963 the Palo Alto scene had spread out, moving in a whirlpool fashion. Willy the Gate went crazy – speed crazy – broke up with Danielle, went to livin' in a garage with some Christmas lights in July, and started to write a great novel, which he later burned on his way to Taos, New Mexico, like Apu throwing away the dream of the great novel and thus being one with God, becoming a Sadhu. At this same time, North Beach was dying out, the San Francisco State College scene was in its infancy and the Palo Alto bunch was starting to scatter.

You must understand there were many madmen around. No two identical. For instance, Joe Novakovich, a mutation, but a bit more obvious. He can uncork wine bottles and beercans well and play the zither. His parents had something to do with Stanford, so Joe was hangin' out when the rest arrived. Garcia and Willy the Gate were sitting there wondering what to do next, so Joe sits down, lends Garcia a guitar and strums along on autoharp.

I suppose Novakovich had more vision than the rest. He knew they would all amount to something someday, albeit not the something mothers boast about. He got around. Berkeley and Sausalito. Palo Alto. LA and Big Sur. Of course, the Chateau. He was absolutely ubiquitous. There he was at the Monterey Jazz Festival, sticking his short fingers into Odduck's candy apple MGA and grinning. What in hell had he to grin about besides common sense and a little faith? Most times he had a little change in his pockets.

In addition to moving around a good deal, Novakovich kept journals and diaries. He wanted to get to the woods to to put all of his notes in order, so he and Laird moved to Los Trancos, a protected country refuge. They lived in a tent up there all winter and damned near died and had fights and drank a lot. Watched the sun and the manzanita peeling away. When they got bored they came down the mountain to Kepler's or St Mike's, and they did all sorts of slightly unsavory things. Like one day Joe and Laird were good and drunk. So they got into an argument as to which was the funkiest. Agreed that the great symbol of funk was how long a pair of boots could be worn without changing socks. They kept a tally. THREE MONTHS LATER, Laird won. Joe felt somethin' crawlin' in his boot – no doubt a mere hallucination. But when they finally took their boots off, the socks were husks of their former argyle. The shrivelly skin was so long gone it didn't smell. But Laird hung his socks out to dry anyway and his toes got some air. As Laird said, 'After three months in your boots there ain't nothin' left to do with your feet 'cept air 'em!'

A few days later, Laird went to get his socks off the line and put 'em back on. But they had strangely hardened. He pulled back to beat them on the tree. Sock falling through void space, the Laird hammer hand driving it on. Ker-slap, it curled around the tree trunk and the cruddy sock promptly disintegrated. Laird and Joe couldn't get their boots on. Their feet said NO, so they went to Los Altos barefoot to take a bath at Joe's house. A nice, long, soaking bath. Joe's mother came home and immediately puckered up.

Joe, what have you killed in your room?

There were other challengers for the FUNKY crown. There was this almost-oriental-looking guy hangin' around

East Pally who had the misfortune to have a rhythm and blues DJ for a father and who was raised hip and lived on T-Bone Walker.

He played fantastic harp, good guitar, and organ riffs, and he played coffee houses around. Sort of fat and quiet and not caring a damn bit about his looks, 'cause there war a lot of folks uglier than him. This was Ron McKernan, later called Pig Pen. In 1968, Laird and Novakovich have a reunion at Pig Pen's house while Pig is on the road. Another fight broke up the whole pad and they throw the empty wine bottles out into the street through the open window (also broken). It never changes.

Pig Pen sometimes worked at Swain's Music Store in Palo Alto. A very young guy named Troy Weidenheimer ran the place for Old Man Swain. Troy tried to get gigs on the side from fraternities and the like and formed a group called the Zodiacs, consisting of Troy on lead, Pig Pen on harp, a whole bunch of different drummers, mostly Bill Kreutzmann, and sometimes no drummer at all, and sometimes Garcia came in on bass.*

Didn't matter much how bad they played since the frat rats were busy getting drunk and hassling the girls. So it was mostly standard rock and roll tunes. Pig Pen made maybe twenty bucks a night for that kind of work. He managed to stay together living with his parents in East Palo Alto. Then again he sometimes went single to parties at St Mike's and the Tangent.

It wasn't until 1964 that Garcia formed *Mother Macree's Uptown Jug Champions*. Which dragged all the loose ends out of the Chateau and haunts of Palo Alto, for awhile at least. Even that was merely a transition. In '62, Pig Pen found himself playing singles again and hitching to Boston for one forlorn mother of a winter until he came home to play for Paul Foster, the Merry Prankster, and Paul Kantner, now in the Jefferson Starship, at the Off-Stage Club in San Jose. It was this bistro that provided nourish-

*The Zodiacs, circa 1962–63, were a fundamental seed for the Grateful Dead. All of the places and people were moving about so fast, although it seemed normal at the time, that a historian could be easily confused.

ment for the grapevine that started to grow rapidly in April 1963.

FADE. NARRATION OVER SHOT OF PSYCHEDELIC BUS CROSSING DESERT.

Paul Foster is not diagnostically mad – a bit hebephrenic, but not mad. He is, however, preoccupied with fantasy. Paul gave the acid tests and Trips Festivals a one-man show and contributed costumes and automatic, egoless laughter. His most remarkable outfit was the mummy: Wrapped in one continuous ace bandage, Paul slipped into a sandwich board which read, 'Are you in the Pepsi generation?' on the front, and 'You're all a bunch of pimply faced teenyboppers' on the back. This outfit also had a number of appendaged appliances, to wit: A cane – white, with red tip – ostensibly for blind, roving mummies, with one addition: This cane had a '55 Buick hood ornament (bombsight) attached to it.

CUT TO DARK HIGH SCHOOL STAGE. SPOT ON PAUL FOSTER, STANDING MOTIONLESS IN SPOTLIGHT, HAIR BEFOULED, BARE FEET CLAD ONLY IN COST-PLUS ZORIS. HE'S WEARING A FUCHSIA-PINK JUMP SUIT, WITH NO UNDERWEAR – AT LEAST NONE WE ARE AWARE OF.

FROM HIS JUMP SUIT ZIPPER, WE SEE A DANGLING MR PEANUT WHISTLE, USED TO PIPE PEOPLE ABOARD; AND IN HIS LEFT HAND WE SEE AN ALLIGATOR CRICKET, USED TO PUNCTUATE THE DISSERTATION.

PAUL SPEAKS IN A COMPUTERIZED, POLYLINGUISTIC STAMMER THAT NO SPEECH PATHOLOGIST COULD EVER DECIPHER:

Well-ll-ll – we gotta get to the bot-t-t-to-om of this thing, this miracle that brought all the fel-l-l-las togeth-ether. And to me, it was simple: It was-ss at the Off-St-St-Stage in San Jose . . . about 1963 . . .

Click
Click
(The alligator clicker)

Da-Da-David Crosby used to come up from Sausalito and-d-d play folk songs . . . to augment his income as a cat burglar.

David Freiberg would team up with a chick named Michaella, and they would-d-d get a lot of laughs.

I was on sp-p-peed at the time – never touch the stuff now – and it wasn't too bad.

A guy named R-Ron Zapowa was the owner, and I r-r-ran it on a profit . . . which blew his mind. Ron is now a bank executive somewhere, but he also started the T-T-Tangent in Palo Alto and brought the s-s-same people over there. Zapowa means 'big wind' in Polish, so he changed his name to Ron Gale – like gale; storm – dig it?

He let Pig Pen play blues, and Pig Pen had a girl from Texas he met on the road named Janis Jo-Jo-Joplin. This was in 1962. Ron would pay Pig and Janis off in money and S-S-Southern Comfort, which Pig t-taugh-taught her how to d-d-drink.

Me – me – personally – I was as-ast-astonished at this whole scene. I spent four years in Fr-France as a computer programmer – then to come into this scene fresh – wow!

Click
Click

One night, Neal Cassady and Allen Ginsberg and W. S. B-Bur-Burroughs came into the Off-Stage with big grins on. They were raving about the legendary m-mother-fucker-marijuana-bush they just planted at Holy City in the Santa Cruz M-Mou-Mountains – above S-S-San Jose. It was gonna be thirty feet in circumference the next year. No-no-nobody knows where it is, but it really exists to th-this d-day, I-I-I'm sure, because they used two pounds of puma shit for f-f-fertilizer.

J-J-Jerry Kaukonen (Jorma Kaukonen) was just graduating from the University of Santa Clara, a Jesuit school, and was also just married to Margarita. He t-t-took to giving lessons in Palo Alto and go-g-going up to play solo, twelve-string blues at the Charles Va-Va-Van Damme in Sausalito. The Van Damme was a mud-wallowing paddlewheeler left over from the ferryboat days before the bridges. First it was Wa-Wa-Juanita's Galley. Then when Wa-Wa-Juanita got busted and got run out of town, it became a worm-eaten eyesore, lis-s-sting to starboard.

Around the f-f-first of 1963, David Freiberg and Dav-Dav-David Crosby went to Venice, California, for awhile to try to live down there and form a group, but it took a l-long time, and Freiberg split back up North. Crosby st-stayed down there and met some other freaks, and they l-later became known as The Byrds. So much for Dav-Dav-David Crosby. He just stay-ay-ayed in LA and made it real big potatoes, while the rest were all starving naked mad and f-f-fucked up in the pits of the estuary, sort of like the Hudson River.

A HUGE BLACK TOP HAT WITH WINGS ATTACHED APPEARS ON STAGE. PAUL STEPS INTO THE HAT. THE HAT REDUCES ITS SIZE AND QUICKLY, IN A FLUTTER, FLIES AWAY, LEAVING ALL SPEECHLESS.

There were guitar players and singers everywhere, but nobody saw very many drummers. A guitar could be packed on a Vespa or could get hitchhiked, but a set of drums was just too much . . . nine boxes and cymbals and sticks and all sorts of extra stuff. So there just weren't too many drummers around. Spencer Dryden was in LA playin' music in studios in the early sixties and there were a lot of jazz drummers around: JAZZ WAS ALL THE RAGE. Jazz was the peak of musicianship in those days, and jazz musicians looked down on folk musicians as city people look down on hillbillies. 'Music is good, but they ain't musicians . . . they can't read a chart.'

But in spite of differences, the merger was taking place,

like world in collision. Jazz was headed directly for folk music, and the explosion had to start in the only place it could – Rock and Roll.

Now there was this real good rock and roll drummer livin' in Palo Alto. He was very strong and used to go up to Perry Lane to take lessons when he was sixteen years old. People had heard of him, but nobody had a band together. This was Billy Kreutzmann, who for some reason changed his name to Sommers for awhile but then later found out that his name meant Man of the Cross, so he changed it back again. People used to call him Bill the Drummer. His dad is an attorney and wanted him to go to Stanford, but he was such a high school dropout he had to go to prep school in Arizona. It didn't matter, as long as he had his drums. His father tried to keep him away from the drums, but it only took one telephone temper tantrum to get the drums on the train to Arizona. Bill has never been separated from his drums since.

He married in 1963 and got a job as a stock clerk at Stanford Research Institute, but he gave drum lessons at Dana Morgan's in his spare time, and that's how he met Garcia and this young kid named Bob Weir. Dana Morgan could play bass, and that was the combo: Dana Morgan on bass, Pig Pen on organ and harp, Garcia lead, Weir rhythm, and Kreutzmann on drums. But, the truth is, nobody really got the combo together until much later. Two full years went by before the Warlocks played at Magoo's.

FLASHBACK
STREETS OF PALO ALTO
1961 – SUMMER

Novakovich and Pig Pen were staunch drinking buddies. One night when the Tangent was really jumping and some cat was wailing away at 'Night Train,' Joe and Pig ran into each other and rolled out to the street to get some wine. Novakovich says:

> **We went out to the lot and met Peter Dema. Pig jumped in a car and pushed the passed-out owner into the back seat.**

We headed for Baronies and just made it before closing. Peter went in and got a quart of Tokay and a quart of white port.

By the time we hit the Tangent, the Tokay was gone, so I slipped the port under my jacket and went in. Almost all, maybe half, of the port went into Pig's beer. We stayed for an hour or so and then split for Pen's place. Harlan, the owner of the car, was still too drunk to drive, so Pig drove. But he was also too drunk and kept running down the wrong side of the road and up onto the sidewalk. 50 mph. Vrrrooomhhh.

We rounded the corner by his house at about 40 and didn't make it. We flashed up over the sidewalk and headed for a truck. Then he managed to get on the lawn and it looked like we would just fit between a tree and the truck. But we hit the truck! Insane! We couldn't stop laughing.

Finally we got the car onto the road and into Pen's. We turned the wheel over to the owner and went inside. Polished off the rest of the wine and laughed near an hour. Then we turned in.

Bambambam. It was the cops and the truck's owner and Harlan. Pig said, 'No, man, I didn't hit the goddamn truck. Whadaya mean wakin' me up at this hour?'

Pig didn't have a license and this was hit and run. He went down the next morning and confessed the whole thing. I guess it pays to be honest . . . he only got a $50 fineJ

FADE.
CUT TO SLOW.
PARTY AT THE CHATEAU SATURDAY NIGHT. HOT AND STILL; EARTHQUAKE WEATHER.

Flamboyant Paul Speegle bids *adieu,* with cape over shoulder and silver-tipped walking cane. Strolls to the car and rides shotgun. '62 Studebaker Golden Hawk with a McCullough Blower. Fast as hell. Overpowered, and we were all afraid of speed, since no one really knew how to drive except for Neal.

Paul, an accomplished painter who was working on a Green Wine run and a series of oils. Blind Prophet. An eerie eyeless sage who peered out at you. Garcia and Paul very close partners.

NO MOON. LOTS OF STARS.

Garcia, who was trying to find himself then and who fancied himself a painter but who could hardly mix mud up right, and lived in the pumphouse with a stash of peanut butter and a banjo, jumped in, too.

Alan Trist the Englishman, with movieblueeyes, seemed to look through you – but really stoned underneath.

And along came Lee Adams to drive Paul home. Laird staggers out onto the wooden porch and shouts:

NO, NO, STOP THEM! IT'S FREAKY!!
But there were taillights down the curves

red streaking
silver ribbons rain
maserati
110
in town

railroad bridge
champion belt
lights
open buckle

open
on peyote and
your car
konks out

right turn to Alpine

spin red and dazed too fast
WOW, IT'S BEAUTIFUL
and the lights go out
until you feel the earth again
soft, the mud ooze.

No moon. Lots of stars.

Noise of Death screeching beyond prayers. Slow-motion collapse and fear, gut-sucking fear.

Pain. Dislocated shoulder. Garcia sets off across the meadow in stocking feet to reach Stanford Hospital.

'Accident'

And points, grunts, gestures until they understand. Wakes up to the sobs and pain from the other room.

PAUL IS DEAD

Garcia senses walls of morphine. Shit, that's death. That's really death, man! And a surge eternal flash all music. Gong gong gong. 'I CAN PAINT WITH MUSIC, EMBROIDER BLUEGRASS, WEAVE IT THROUGH THOUSANDS OF LAYERS IN BETWEEN I'M DEAD' (ONCE DEAD NOW ALIVE). Gurdjieffian joy of awareness. Golden lotus from mud rising.

After Paul Speegle's death, Garcia started to look like Claude Debussy. Thin facial features, goatee, and a mole exactly in the same place where Debussy had a mole. Phil noted this immediately upon seeing him at the Chateau. There he was, reincarnated: Claude Debussy hatching an unfinished symphony, but more likely trying to perfect his ability as a performer. Garcia can do more than anybody. He can force himself to play for hours on end, almost like Ali Akbar Khan. He had always played guitar, but not fervently . . . now it was as if death and fire had ignited a chemical reaction.

By 1963 there began to be little community houses of friends that Bob Hunter strung together with his pollenating back and forth. One was on Gilman Street. A group formed called the Hart Valley Drifters, and before that, the Thunder Mountain Tub Thumpers. Dave Nelson played guitar, Garcia banjo, Bob Hunter string bass, and a guy named Ken Frankel mandolin. They entered the Monterey Folk

Festival competition in the amateur bluegrass category and won.

The Hart Valley Drifters became the even more ridiculous Mother Macree's Uptown Jug Champions, or the Asphalt Jungle Boys. It didn't matter much, since almost everybody that was in Palo Alto at the time sat in. Dave Parker, who is now the Dead's accounts manager, played washboard. Bob Matthews, who is now the head of Alembic Studios and Electronics Corp., played jug; and a little guy named Marmaduke, who is now the lead for the New Riders of the Purple Sage, sang and played guitar.

All of that seems remote. The once-lean Garcia now looks like a Basque. Round shoulders, blue denim shirt, cowboy boots, face covered with beard and hair, poncho warming and hiding all the good food-stuffs, glasses from the eye doctor in LA, back cracked by Dr Fritz, and two kids. When I describe him as a Basque, I make reference to the very clever tenet set forth by Ignatius Donnelly in his early work on Atlantis. From this we see that Iberio-Keltic peoples were probably the first, and most direct descendants of the foundering Atlantis. Now, in Jerry's case his father was pure Spanish (IBERIAN) and his mother pure Irish (KELTIC). He looks Spanish but thinks like an Irishman and is, by this reduction, probably an Atlantean.

In the early fifties, Jerry's father, Joe, was a band leader, a good band leader at that. He played clarinet and flute and alto saxophone and, ironically, held dances at a big dance hall out by Playland, later to become the last Family Dog . . . but he fell overboard and drowned on a fishing trip, when Jerry and Tiff (his older brother) were very young. At that time, they were mostly living with their grandmother in one of the family homes in the Excelsior District of San Francisco (Outer Mission), a house that was homesteaded before the Earthquake and Fire of '06. Jerry's mom owned a bar downtown under the freeway near the Bay Bridge and that's where Jerry and Tiff hung out a lot; sometimes they would live in the Claremont Arms Apartments behind the bar, and sometimes they would stay with Grandma Clifford.

Eventually, Jerry's mom, Ruth Clifford-Garcia, married a guy named Wally Matuzowitz and moved down the Peninsula. Wally managed the bar and commuted each day in his Cadillac until the place was sold to the State of California for a freeway entrance. In other words, Jerry had bars and bistros and music in his blood from birth, so it is no wonder that he gave in so completely. It's almost like a Jack London story. It was Jerry's destiny to play whatever form of music he could master, in the San Francisco tradition.

This same traditional destiny holds true for Phil and Pig Pen. Phil's grandfather was a bandmaster for a summer civic band in Ohio, much like Charles Ives. Pig Pen's dad had more than a slight familiarity with the blues in his capacity as an early rhythm and blues disc jockey.

Bob Weir, on the other hand, took an early and precocious liking to the guitar, much to the dismay of his family; and Kreutzmann, well, he had too much energy. He's even got his kid banging on pots and pans.

FLASH BACK TO 1962

The Chateau actually became the center of everything for awhile. People from everywhere started to drop in. The whole scene had become one giant party after another, kicked off and sort of melted together by the GROOVY CONCLAVE. November 18, 1961, 9:30 p.m.

The idea was to invite everybody far enough in advance to get everyone there. And it worked. This Conclave went on for three days. Wild drunken brawls, with no bad vibes, no LSD, just booze and music and grass and maybe a speed freak or two. It was still a black-and-white party, a salt-and-pepper party. The tone was black and white, but the raciality was transcendental. Just a bunch of horny beatniks. Nobody cares anyway.

The invitations to the Groovy Conclave were actually mimeographed, and hundreds were distributed. Half moon tilted to the north on the horizon about 20° and an eerie drone coming from the house. Danny Barnett's big old weird truck with the torn front seat marking the driveway, and John the Cool's little old weird pickup in front of the wooden porch. Both of them seemed like rusty hulks in the moonlight. Every room in the house was jammed from stem to stern, and the whole place reminded one of an abandoned square-rigger that had been reinvested with old ghosts.

The most unique feature of the Chateau was the poker room, which was really the central hub of the house. Jim Carico, the artist, hid in the small niche off the kitchen and was thus in touch with everybody. There were hardly any rugs, so the wooden floors and linoleum creaked a lot from the foot traffic. Sandals, bare feet, motopsycho boots, tennis shoes, cowboy boots, blue suede brogans, and alligator shoes, huarachis with rubber-tire tread soles, even an occasional nylon-clad foot would sneak through late at night. One thing for certain: it wasn't no dress-up theatrical trip. Everybody came specifically to get ripped with his friends, and that's why it was called the Groovy Conclave.

Bob Hunter calculated maybe three or four hundred people showed up. Rod Albin and the Boar's Head Coffee House people came, and Rod set about giving everyone Allport-Vernon-Lindzey Value questionnaires. Odduck was in the upstairs somewhere, having a fanatic discussion about the hinges of history. Phil was chasing broads and wenching about. Garcia was singin' and pickin' in the front room, and so it went for three whole dimly lit crashpad mindless daze. Poker games in between, for diversification.

A contingent from Santa Clara showed up consisting of Jorma Kaukonen and his pals from the newly begun Off-Stage. The Fariñas and the Big Sur bunch showed up; Roy Seburn, still trying to shake the motorcyle club in Burlingame (The Burlingame Spiders appeared and then went back to Homer Lane to get a busload). Neal and about six furry little honeys darted in, rumbled up in front in an old La Salle four-door sedan with a torn headliner. Neal just pointed 'em toward the door and said SHOO. They scattered about the rooms and were absorbed like capillary action.

It was honest poverty.

Women liked you because you were good lookin' or you laid the right rap on 'em or because they loved your mind and wanted your body . . . not because you were a famous somebody, not because you were a rock star, not because you had bread. That's the *new* scene. That's the present degenerate value system. In those days it was simply because you fired up some kundalini and they responded.

The Groovy Conclave was a precursor to the Acid Tests, but not quite. No one was precisely aware of history yet. The average age at that party was twenty-two, counting Neal and the other old farts, and there wasn't any desperation. Everybody had it 'knocked,' as the phrase goes. Almost everybody.

The Chateau went on until about late 1963.

Amorphous journal fragment dated simply April. No day, no year. Possibly attributed to Novakovich, circa 1963:

Today was about as uncreative as a day can be. I sat around St Mike's for a little time and then wandered off to Dana's and tuned a few autoharps. Pig came in about 4:00 and we decided that after 'work' we'd go down to Ingram's and get some food and wine. It was a long walk but there was nothing else to do. So around 6:00 off we went.

We bought a quart of white wine, four bagels and one-half pound of salami for a grand investment of $1.64 and off we went to the 'drinkin' ' place up by El Camino Real, a bit beyond the underpass on University Avenue. We crawled up to the bushes and ate and drank in peace. When we came out and started walking down the street a voice from the street said 'You'd better hurry!' We looked and there was Dez Perado, alias Page Browning, sitting in his car. As soon as I opened the door, a sweet, wonderful smell came rollicking into my nostrils. POT! 'Whee!' says Pig, and away we went.

Later at the Tangent, Pig asked me what had happened to Al Lober – the Great Existentialist, hero of postwar America. Al Lober, who drove dragsters in Detroit and all the way to New Orleans without stopping to eat or sleep but only for gas. And who is now in Oaxaca eating sacred mushrooms.

After the Tangent, Pig and I cut out to eat hash browns and scrambled eggs at Dink's Donuts. Wow! Too much! I tell Pig about a concert and party in San Jose at the Off-Stage. I wonder what will happen there. I think I'll go

see. I also wonder what will become of Pig. I worry about him. He's kinda helpless sometimes. , . .

I'm buying French fries in Brewer's. I think I'll eat them and go to Dana Morgan's Music Store. Jerry is having a concert towards the end of April with Mike Seeger. He's also getting married to Sarah sometime soon. (Sugaree?)

I got a brochure from the Monterey Folk Festival today. The thing sounds great. New Lost City Ranblers, Clarence

I got a brochure from the Monterey Folk Festival today. The thing sounds great. New Lost City Ramblers, Clarence Ashley, Doc Watson, Roscoe Holcomb, and Garcia and Dave Nelson and Hunter are in the bluegrass contest. Too much! I think I'll go down. It has potentials for a scene. Inexpensive food, hoots, workshops, lectures and all sorts of people. Joan Baez wants anyone who needs a place to come out to her house in the Highlands. Maybe I'll take her up on it. Sure would be groovy. Early morning hills of sunrise, Pacific Ocean, and the mist and rain of a million lifetimes.

I need money. I may have to borrow at least $15.00 from Pig until someone buys my dulcimer or until I get another job. Henry Miller once ran an ad with his picture saying 'I need money.' I wish I could do that and get as much as he did.

Maybe I'll go down to LA and look up David Crosby. I hear he's got one hell of a rock and roll group together. Haven't heard from him in a long time, so he must be up to no good. He was always a Sausalito scoundrel, hangin' out with Ale Ekstrom and the concertina crowd at Gate Six.

Next entry, still dated April. Maybe this guy only wrote in his diary in April each year. The Palo Alto scene was easily that amnesiac. Had to be at least '63, though. The following mention of Janis Joplin tells a tale:

I'm singing at Coffee and Confusion, formerly The Fox and the Hound, a coffee hoot club on Grant Avenue in North Beach. I'm playin' my little guitar riff and in walks Janis Joplin. Her eyes were bulgin' out and she was funky

drunk, but she sang with me and we had a good time. Then she invites me over to her pad to stay the night. She lives on Page Street in the Haight-Ashbury with a guy named George the Beast (George Howell) and others I never met. Stayed for three days, then headed back to Palo Alto on bus. Hate to go through the San Francisco Greyhound Terminal. Bad place to be happy in; bad place to turn on your third eye.

Arrive in Palo Alto and run into Pig on the street first thing. He sez: 'Come on, man, you're gonna need a drink for this. I got somethin' to tell ya'.' I told him I didn't need no drink, but he said I would, so we have a big snort of vodka and he tells me Sally Dema just died the night before in an auto accident on the Skyline.

He was right. I had been with her cute little self last week. So we gets drunk beyond reprieve. Peter Dema drunk too.

The Chateau was a good thing. I'm sorry Sally and Paul Speegle didn't get to see more of it. The parties up there used to go on for days. Wonderful parties, beautiful people. But now they're all gone. The great party pad and home for wayward artsy types has gone for a Baptist Church.

I guess about everyone with Bohemian tendencies that ever came to Palo Alto went to a party or lived at the Chateau, and in the six or seven years it was going, the police were only up three or four times. One time I remember clearly, about 1960 or so. Sue Mayberry was going with Page Browning. She would come to the parties on a Friday night with her overnight bag and burst open the door and scream at the top of her lungs, 'Hi! I'm here for the party! Woooow! Gimme something to drink!' That was a joke; she never drank – just blew pot and took pills. Anyway she would usually leave on Sunday, to return again next Friday. But not this time. Her parents got wise and sent the cops out after her. We hid her in a tree behind the pump shack. But the cops found her, and when they asked her what she was doing, she said she was an owl and to go away. Then she went 'Whooo' and stuck her tongue out at them. They went away. For some unknown reason they went away. Nobody was uptight in those days. It was like a dream.

Just a few years ago, everybody's dream was just to get laid a lot and have a lot of grass and not get busted, and try to live from your talents. And it was with this value in mind that Alan Trist threw a party while his father (who was linked to a social science thinktank at Stanford) was away. The pad was nice, and Alan was advanced over the rest of us because of his European education, which allowed him more freedom of movement in the social circus.

The party unexpectedly ended when Dr Trist came home to find this mad BEER CAN scene, balling in the closet, and Novakovich doin' it under the hors d'oeuvres table and bumping the closet door shut on Phil, likewise indisposed.

rancid Marlboro smoke and stale beer
turkoman tattooed against the comatose and
naked forms. TV on all night.

AALLLLLANNN! OH BUGGAH. When Alan's father got to the bedroom and saw Heath Moon disporting pleasantly upon embossed percale with his motorcycle boots on . . . naturally all the celebrants left hurriedly.

Alan and his father had a talk, and it was decided that Alan and his friend Dan Eaves would take a long hike up into the mountains. The John Muir Trail was a very California place to go.

The Muir trail extends from Yosemite in mid-state to Mount Whitney in the south . . . a distance of 427 miles or so, and only the most intrepid try it. But intrepid trips are a local specialty.

Thus we find Alan and his friend assailing a ridge of the Sierra. Dusk came, but they had to keep going, as it was too steep to camp. The map showed a cabin or ranger station at the top. They had to get out the flashlight and walk by its light. It gets dark up in the Big Woods. Suddenly there was this drunken shout from the middle of nowhere:

What the fuck ya' doin' out here with a flashlight?

They stumbled and tripped through the underbrush toward the voice.

Hallo, gentlemen. Allow me to introduce myself. Neal Cassady.

And there he was . . . a tent and a chick; a donkey, right in the middle of . . .

Ya' know some of my friends in Palo Alto? Too much! Here's my phone number. Get some sleep.

Dawn came. Neal had gone. Never even heard the car. And that's how Alan met Neal. It is similar to how EVERYBODY met Neal, at random, through some commodious synchronicity.

There was nothing to do but study and go to parties and part the seas and gulp down barrels of tragedy and giggle a lot. And it should be obvious that there is a fine line between this fantasy and the early follies. Will we learn the difference? Will we hit it big in the next kalpa? Who knows? It's funny how the tribal dream shifts around. It's strange how the Grateful Dead tribal dream is identical to thousands of others.

BERKELEY

We have only one effective weapon:
The power to blow their minds.

– Mario Savio

Occasionally, in the alchemy of history, perhaps only once each generation, a homunculus is brought forth that grows into a man of extreme magical power. Often, however, this man realizes not his magic and falls to earth. Less common is the man who realizes his magic and responds to it with zeal, only to find himself ensconced in his vanity, unable to rise above time and the material body. The rarest of all events is a man who has realized his magic and has set about to see himself lead a divine existence regardless of the tariff on such an act, regardless of such torments and antipathy as he would most assuredly encounter in the course of his life. Such a man was Paracelsus, as was Hermes Thrice Great, Jesu, the Lord Gautama, and the thousands of secret masters that have gone unnoted.

Ken Kesey had a friend who came close to being aware of the true magic, an alchemist who thought of himself as Merlin is a short guy with a reasonably high IQ, who happened to migrate from LA to Berkeley about 1962. Someone convinced him that Berkeley was where the scene was at.

Merlin started out making methedrine in 1965, and then LSD in 1966. He got a 'rep,' a mystique, he ran the press wild . . . *King of Acid*, they called him. He acted mysterious appeared and disappeared, hung out with the Grateful, Dead, then the Jefferson Airplane, then Moby Grape, Blue Cheer, then the intellectual set . . . everyone had a different view. The kids on Haight Street and Telegraph Avenue thought he was akin to a god.

1ST STREET PERSON: Got his lab cut loose
Got hisself cut loose, too.

	Went right out and made a bunch more dope. Yessir!
2ND STREET PERSON: (BEGGING FOR 'SPARE CHANGE')	Merlin never got it to the final stages until the last minute so that if they busted in on him there was nothin' to bust but dust.
1ST STREET PERSON:	Finally got him on 24 counts of running an illegal laboratory or somethin'. BDAC got him, but not until he turned on 15 million people, most of 'em more 'n once. Hee, hee!
2ND STREET PERSON:	Sticking to one goal: To turn on everyone in the world, every sentient human being, at least once. Would take one cubic ton of pure LSD.

But Merlin was, in point of fact, a late-comer to the scene. Lots of LSD was around in sugar cubes, and from IFIF and Sandoz, many years before Merlin arrived in Berkeley.

Merlin got started in chemistry one day when Barbara Brown Shoe, who lived at the Brown Shoe Commune, took him over to Room 292 in the Biological Sciences Building at Berkeley.

That's it over there – the lab. Come on in with me, Merlin, you'll dig it.

They sneaked in the corridor and up and down. The wonders never cease: There was Melinda, standing in the laboratory, foxy as hell, and with that 200 IQ, and Merlin and her began to rap, so Barbara had to cut out and leave them alone. The rap had to do with optical isomers of essential oil of parsley and buckeye poison, and ultimately LSD, which grossed him millions but netted him nothing.

Merlin's concept of wealth was akin to the Worm Ouroboros, the primal religion. The idea is to enhance 'immortality' honestly attained – not to beg for it . . . not to control your mystique . . . not to buy friends.

NEWSPAPER MAN: (1970)	**What's your relationship to Merlin?**
GARCIA:	Well, Merlin is in and out of jail and Merlin is our friend and that's all he's ever been, really. And because he's a difficult cat, we're probably the only friends he has, or among the few friends he has.
NEWSPAPER MAN:	**You did a benefit for him?**
GARCIA:	Yes, and we'll probably do some more too because he can sure use the money now that he has a possibility of getting out. And he really doesn't deserve to be in jail. A real friend will tell you when you're out of line. A false friend simply syrups compliments on a weak ego.

Merlin would often panic his friends, and even scare himself, but he had an inner sense of right-on-ness, and everyone he had ever met felt he was the guy who really knew where IT was at. Merlin always seemed to be driven by an inner power, or a personal power, which he alone had access to.

David Crosby said:

I thought I knew a man who knew a man who knew the truth!

It doesn't take long for a guy like Merlin to get a hero cult started. He was so fantastically sure of himself that nobody disbelieved him – not at first, anyway.

The private view of Merlin is considerably different from the public view he has developed, or that has been developed for him. He never learned that a reporter will always says something dumb if you don't tell him what to say. Part of Merlin's mystique was this quality of veiled secrecy, this I-have-the-answer attitude. No matter how fantastic the rap got, everyone believed him. No matter how much acid you dropped to keep up with him, he would always isolate himself, To most people he preferred this pedestal.

Merlin's influence was global, yet the first global experience was the assassination of President Kennedy, and it was a bummer.

Odduck was at San Francisco State in a criminology class when somebody came screaming down the hall –

THE PRESIDENT HAS BEEN SHOT!
SOMEBODY SHOT THE PRESIDENT!

The student body stood numb in the fog, waiting, listening for more news, amidst tears and sobs.

Odduck put it succinctly:

The 'fact' of the President's murder was disgusting, but worse was the shock that he was 'our' President. Some students actually had clung to the belief that the government was at least partially representative of even our poor dumb, miserable asses. The murder of our personal hero could have been rationalized. Presidents have been assassinated before. But what really fucked us up – the Bohemian youth – was the covering up of the covering up of the demi-murders . . . the White House whitewash of

the Jack Ruby, Martin Luther King, Bobby Kennedy murders. With each new assassination and disappearance and cancer we got a little tougher and more hateful. I saw my friends turn from the idyllic artist types to surly I-hate-the-world types. Everyone seemed to regress to barbarism to gross out the people who let the assassins go undetected. Incidentally, not a man among us believes Oswald did it alone but we do believe we know who did, and 'they' are still walking around on this planet with guns and poison and a truck-like motivation to purify Amerika.

In 1962, most of the political rhetoric seemed to emanate from Berkeley. But there were two scenes in Berkeley, as if there were two dissociative personalities fighting inside one organism: the music-drug scene and the political-drug scene. The politicals didn't have much use for dope at first, and the artist types did. It was only later that guys like Jerry Rubin found hedonism a perfect political platform; it was only later that the Orgy League got undulating.

But LSD didn't really come on strong until 1965, and even then there was no tragedy in LSD and mescaline and pot as long as one was involved in a sincere search. In short, after LSD, everything was color; prior to LSD, everything was a cruddy black-and-white schmaze.

About 1959, the House Unamerican Activities Committee (HUAC) convened in San Francisco. HUAC was left over from the McCarthy era and was empowered to go on a witch hunt when and if it deemed the national interests could profit from gouging a few Communists and dupes of Communists and the sympathizers of the dupes.

A is A; therefore A
A tautological fallacy:

If you are not a Communist, you must be a dupe of the Communists unless you are against the Communists. 'If you ain't with us – yer with them.' How do you actually know you ain't in the CIA? You might be drafted in your sleep. A dupe is anyone who doesn't hate Communists as much as HUAC!

The same Communism paranoia that threatened avant garde San Francisco Bohemians back in the 1930's, like Izzy Gomez, William Saroyan, Dalton Trumbo and Upton Sinclair, returned in 1959 in the form of HUAC.

The big, colossal city hall, with its Versailles-like façade, its dome actually bigger than the one in Sacramento, but pale green, was housing the HUAC meetings. So naturally everybody split from all around to see the show. Malvina Reynolds was there, singing; and Ira Sandoyster and his nineteen-year-old friend, Joan Baez, got up and sang and gave a speech.

Then everybody moved inside the city hall and up the marble steps and sat in the various vestibules to protest the very existence of HUAC, and that's when the mayor ordered the late Chief Ahern to turn on the hoses.

Bumpitty.

.

.Bumpitty.

.

.Bump.

.

.down the slide flew many of the City's best demonstrators. This hosing outraged the socialist community, and it took to marching about town in pairs or in rallies of twenty or so for months after, carrying signs reading DOWN WITH BOURGEOISIE WASTELAND! and KILL THE WITCH-HUNTERS! Next week, the Nazis retaliated by throwing a bomb into the doorway of the rather benign Coexistence Bagel Shop. This only served to give poets like Bob Kaufman an even bigger sense of unreality.

Still, the poetry got better.

Small cliques formed into coalitions – some just to live together, but others to plot anarchy. There was a faction of soft Socialist Trotskyites and a faction of hard Stalinists in town, and they never saw eye to eye.

In 1964, from the Stalin-Trotsky conflict, the W. E. B. Du Bois Club was formed . . . a quickening Maoist cell in the heart of the Fillmore ghetto on McAllister Street, wedged in between antique stores and rummage lofts. The club had a storefront meeting hall and a semisecret downstairs grotto that threw parties hosted by the Hallinans – K. O., Dynamite, etc.

'The Boys Club' also had some active unknowns like Tracy. Tracy Simms was a hypermanic black woman who shot back and forth between Berkeley and S.F. State. She discovered, for lack of agitation, that the Sheraton Palace was not hiring blacks, or at least not enough, so the Du Bois Club threw a small demonstration which got out of proportion fast. It went on for three days . . . all night long and all day the next day, and the next. It became another rally for the people 'to see what we've got,' as Tracy described it.

Caught with their pants down, the NAACP had to show up in force and join with the Du Bois Club. Then the papers got on the bandwagon and the crowd swelled. I remember hearing firecrackers go off in the midst of the mob and wondering if this hadn't been an experiment to cause a riot.

In two days, the Sheraton Palace got to be the 'in' place to be. All the liberal dignitaries dropped by for a pace around the picket lines. Ferlinghetti came and stayed and talked to Hallinan. He split. Alan Watts and Ralph Gleason showed up, scuffled around a bit; then they split. It was actually cats like John Handy who stayed all night and on.

Finally, on the third evening, some people actually 'sat in' in the palatial foyer of the hotel. Bodies and newspapers and street clothes appear in this formal sanctum – pregnant chicks and babies and lunch bags. And that's when the people started getting rank. Old ladies in the hotel attacked with umbrella vengeance, janitors (white) spat on the kids. Hardly anybody had any grass, and it was no fun. The cops made up their collective MIND to do something and about twenty-five people were busted.

San Francisco State was politically off-beat. There was action, but it was nihilistic and unmotivated. It wasn't until everything had already come and gone that good ol' S.F. State took the cake.

LAP DISSOLVE TO SHOT OF TAC SQUAD MOVING IN ON HERD OF BLEATING SHEEP. FALL OF 1968.

HEADLINES: STATE CAMPUS CLOSED SEVEN MONTHS.

Some sort of record one could guess!

In the early 1960's, fraternities dominated the rap: free speech meant everybody screamed all at once, and the frats got drunk, gang-banged, tortured, hazed and initiated themselves out of existence. (They still exist, but as mere husks of their former Episcopalian arrogance.)

The frat rats and sorority Sallys started to take acid and smoke pot under the protective wing of the house mother. Their trips were rarely bad, and they often managed a typically macabre sense of humor. For instance, some mountain climber managed to get Mickey Mouse hands attached to the campanile clock on the Berkeley campus. This was sheer artistry. The guy had to climb out over the roof in broad daylight to do it. The hands stayed on the clock for three weeks.

The campanile was called Suicide Tower. 1963 saw murders and mad violence on the Berkeley campus, crimes of passion, maniac Arabs spritzing the library with 22-caliber bullets, shotgun blasts in the Chancellor's office (not politically motivated – just bizarre).

Weedless Berkeley was a highly contrasted place in the early 1960's. Dick and Mimi Fariña would play at the Cabal, a night club, and Joan Baez was around . . . short black hair and the guitar case, not really too radical, not really too political, but funky and free and careless and hopeful. Musically speaking, a real folk singer. Big Sur hot baths and concerts at Dietjen's Inn.

Joan, Kim and Mimi helped alleviate my fears. They sowed the seeds of euphoria to come. It was not so much their state of mind, as beset by the symptoms of national decay as my own, but their ability to satirize the superpatriots, who were in all likelihood our common foe-men. Each of them possessed an accomplished actress's ear for the commonplace, an ability to affect manner and inflection, which rendered the objective source ridiculous. Going out to

dinner became less a method of satisfying hunger than an opportunity for the public assumption of middle-class roles. To ease our mortal anxiety over atrocities in Birmingham, Strontium 90 in baby teeth, Barry Goldwater's photoelectric flagpole (Stars and Stripes triggered by the light of a rising Arizona sun), we could not put aside the vaguely hysterical need to change personality gears. Joan became Lois Faceless, wife and mother; Kim became Harriet Paralysis, cafeteria hostess; Mimi was Midge Motionless, Parcheesi queen of Kansas City; I was Fred Hodaddy, amateur golf champion; and so on.

Richard Fariña

Here, it is plain to see, was their need to wipe out the old *masque du culture* and replace it with one of such ludicrousness that it was rendered forever useless. The temptation to be serious about Mom and Dad would never recur completely.

Thus people like Dick Fariña chose to grow up synthetically (absurdly) rather than stay feeble, ineffectual, and passive to the atrocities they saw.

The early sixties were wooden years in Berkeley. Electronics were nowhere around, except perhaps in the corners of minds of such people as Phil, Morton Sobotnik and Luciano Berio. The dominant purity of life was the acoustic guitar and the Big Sur straight track.

Sather Gate was still a street – bronze green gate at the end, little shops, K. O. Hallinan slate party, soap box near Ludwig's fountain.

Ludwig was the finest example of his breed extant. In those days Ludwig, the German shorthair pointer, would hold forth in his fountain on Sproul Plaza, entertaining the troops of demonstrators, diving for sandwiches, pulling people into the pool and hanging around for about six hours a day. As long as Ludwig was in his fountain there were no riots. But the world has only a few Ludwigs, and his master matriculated.

About 1964, the Free Speech movement – the Mario Savio movement – the Ramparts Magazine movement – the Jerry

Rubin movement – and the Grateful Dead, AKA the Zodiacs, AKA Mother Macree's Uptown Jug Champions, AKA Pig Pen, AKA Sarah and Jerry, AKA the Warlocks – got started. The folk music trip went back and forth from the Cabal in Berkeley to the Tangent in Palo Alto, from the Off-Stage Club in San Jose to the Van Damme ferryboat in Sausalito – the street gypsy troubadors made it on guts alone, and the Grateful Dead family started incubating a huge egg, a huge, brightly colored cascarone for the next celebration: the celebration of truth through fire, the ordeal of LSD, before anyone.

The Troll knew about truth. As a poet he was a marvelous street theologian. If his nose twitched, it was absolute. Long generations of rune reading and Norwegian stargazing led to this talent – the nose twitches, the truth is told: an aurora borealis of truth smelling. Even the small wart on the end of the thing, of the bulb of the thing, twitched. This nose, snub and hard, was all that he had to get him through the crimes of life. The Troll had moved to Berkeley to live off the book-theft trade for a time.

The Troll was a symbolic friend and dwarf companion to marauders as they strode through the underworld in search of fresher air. He had blond hair, slicked back like a convict, stuck down with pomade, like a blood; cut short at the ends. Fresh, ready to fight, shoulders sloped down. He was not a midget – rather a dwarf-folk. Fully a man, but compacted. Not even truncated, simply proportional. But loudly meaner than catshit, and meaner than anybody. If we wanted to see meanness, to trip out with a mean guy, we hung out with Troll. He always balanced out the squares who crept into parties. He hated the unfaithful types who defrauded the gods of sincerity because they made a habit of giggling in the face of tragedy and dishonoring compassion.

The Troll was a night-creeper, and furtive. He and Phil got into a triad woman-hassle, acting out, in Berkeley, the cardinal gothic ritual . . . the famous squaw-theft machismo number. Phil, feeling hurt, sulked for awhile but realized the humor of it and made it over and over again with music as a proper mistress, while Troll took his freshly stolen lady on the rails with him . . . go bum again! Got busted on a security check in New York, and his lady friend had to sell peyote buttons to spring him. But more of the Troll later.

The Las Vegas Strip hides the slum on the north side (The Side) and the middle-class dealers, show girls and pit bosses live on the Hoover Dam side. It all glows together; the dust infests everything, push rods jam out through the sides of 1958 Chevrolets, the heat and sand eat up water pumps; even Volkswagens gasp a last breath cursing at Rommel's impossible Sahara. At night the town can be seen from miles out, near Barstow. An infinite waterless waste – and there, right in the middle, a spa of sorts, full of prairie chiggers and junkies and perverts and tourists off to catch a ten-day thrill. And half-beaten pawnbrokers still gambling, and all of the children of the hotel and the Air Force industry, and the Valley of Fire Indian sacred places and Yagé place.

And there are a few smart guys there, too. One of them is/was Tom Constantin, son of a maître d'hôtel at the Sahara. 'Knows Frank Sinatra.' And a high-class mother with Empire furniture, in and out of an ecstatic oxygen tent to swig a little wine and dote a bit on Tom and the other brother, who were both geniuses.

His brother, a mesomorph, has no pimples and plays football, but is slightly afraid to get his brains kicked into his ass and now goes on a fellowship to Cal Tech. He designed a laser beam right there in Las Vegas, an improved version when he was sixteen, underneath his choo-choo train set.

Tom had his first symphony performed when he was sixteen, which means he wrote it when he was about twelve or thirteen. But he quickly tired of Las Vegas, thought he'd cut up a bit in Berkeley, and so, with or without Moms Persimmon, he set about to clunk the Oldsmobubble up the highway North to catch a glimpse of Mensa and other galaxies at Berkeley. Had astronomy mastered . . . had a big white telescope, a huge stash of mismatched sox, and a 170 IQ.

On campus, in the Music Department some weeks later, while going through a tone test which all music majors must take, Tom overheard Phil talking about atonal music, and because they both had perfect pitch, they struck it off right away.

Tom proposed that Phil attend Luciano Berio's symposium at Mills College. This was more exciting than school anyway, so Phil dropped out and took to composing full-time and going to Berio's classes and swiping books and getting high and engineering at KPFA and cruising over to Palo Alto to catch the parties at the Chateau, Litton Street, the Peace Center, and Perry Lane. That's when he taped Garcia.

1962 went by, and Phil and Tom were gettin' itchy to follow Berio to Europe for a summer tour. Tom proposed that they repair to Las Vegas and live at his house and work at the post office to earn enough to finance the trip. As it turned out, Tom's mother hated Phil and kicked him out, blaming him for Tom's eccentricities. Things seemed like a jungle again. Tom traveled to Europe with Berio and left Phil to work his way back from Las Vegas. Naturally, Phil headed straight for Palo Alto.

Later that year, when Tom got back from Europe, he made many trips to Phil's place in the City. By the spring of 1963 they had decided to find an apartment and compose together. Bill Walker was riding back and forth from Las Vegas, too, and Odduck was living nearby on Twin Peaks and settled down to college after getting busted and divorced a couple of times.

Steve Reich, whom Phil and Tom had met in Berio's class was working on electronic pieces and introduced Phil to the San Francisco Mime Troupe, a group of left-wing weirdos who decided to form a satirical repertoire company as a front for whatever other activities went on. Alvin Duskin and the people from Emerson College in Monterey would pop in from time to time with money and suggestions.

The Mime Troupe was a godsent fulcrum in the San Francisco underground. Ronnie Davis attracted a bunch of creative people and promoters and performers such as were eventually part of the original Community, and that's another Palo Alto connection, since the Peace Center and Joan Baez and Dick and Mimi Fariña were often doing things with the mime people. They held DaDa happenings, action theater, and electronic music shows.

Stewart Brand, who later developed the total environment

trips, festivals and the Whole Earth Catalog, was also greatly obvious at mime troupings.

A sample program follows:

Steve Reich

Proportional Piece #1
Pitch Chart #2
Pitch Chart #1

Phil Lesh

6 7/8 for Bernardo Moreno

A Solo Mime by Danny McDermott

Gwenn Watson

J. S. Bach, Suite #3 in C Major
for unaccompanied cello

Tom Constantin

Piano Piece #3
Free improvisations
on a harp board

The performances were usually held at the old church on Kapp Street in the Mission District, but they also might be held in the parks or on college campuses.

The Mime Troupe produced a number of difficult existential plays, some written locally, like 'Chorizo'; and some more classical, such as 'Ubu Roi' and 'Tartuffe.' The plays were promoted and managed by a young businessman who had dreams of being a promoter, a Dadaist in his own way – Bill Graham! (Small world, ain't it?)

Because of their avant garde European flavor and the obvious 'Guerrilla Theater,' the Mime Troupe was not financially successful as Graham had hoped. He found himself a capitalist in a den of 'Wobblies.' In those days everyone was much more into producing art objects and performing spontaneously than getting rich.

It's still that way for the Grateful Dead, and Mr. Graham still wants to unseat Sol Hurok. What really changes?

During the golden period of the Mime Troupe, Phil worked for the post office driving a truck on a pickup route. He starved until he got that job, and he got it because of his employment record (good) in Las Vegas.

Tom Constantin also worked for the post office, but Tom was employed sorting and bagging international mail at the Ferry Building. We were all so proud of Tom at the time. There he was, sorting federal mail and making sure that all mail addressed to the Narcotics Division of the Treasury Department got sent to American Samoa. Later Tom went back and joined the Air Force and made Airman of the Month. He said his secret was to volunteer for everything!? This led him to scientology.

After a few post office months, Phil's hair grew long and he refused to cut it. It was short by present standards, but the supervisors had no relative futuristic vision: it must be cut off. Phil went to the line with it, then quit when the heat got too bad. That is the irony of it all. Only a short time ago a guy was being harassed for having a Beatle haircut (1964) and now every longhair who can get in, works at Rincon Annex. A full 25 percent of the San Francisco underground action is financed by the federal government through the post office. They say that during coffee breaks you can smell Rincon a mile away. Everybody runs up to the roof to smoke. Ah, progress!

NORTH BEACH

He was very tired after his trip. He ordered a light supper, consisting of nothing but suckling pig, ate it, undressed immediately, climbed under his blanket, and went to sleep. He slept deeply, wonderfully, as only the fortunate can sleep, who know nothing of hemorrhoids, lice or overdeveloped mental faculties.

– Gogol
Dead Souls

San Francisco was terribly depressing and excruciatingly beautiful in those street days. The freedom was one big existential fart in the void.

By 1962, everyone had discovered through some satori, or through some gutter-wallowing, that marijuana, or its equivalent, was the glue that held the world together. The street people all sort of realized that not only was grass good for ya' when ya' got some of it, it was medicine . . . not just for beatniks in the alleys and lofts, but for Arabs and college professors and doctors.

Just down from North Beach was Chinatown . . . innocent tourist-trap Chinatown. But the tourist front was just a put-on:

We jus' little China peeple – no tlubble.
You likee fiaclackah?

Why do you never see a cop in Chinatown? Chinese guys too short. Chinese police force would be a dwarf force, with very little to police, since the 'Tongs' had it under control. On hot nights, you can hear the rattling of Mah-Jongg ivory in the back flats, and the little windows with the hum of sewing machines and the sweat/steam laundries . . . run on opium.

Laird once saw an old Chinese cat with a bucketful of opium pipes in a basement, and the other old dudes laid out like that, and knew it was really China, not Chinatown.

You could always tell the old Buddhist stoners and you could always tell when there was some 'mud' in town. The old cats were strung out and never thought of shooting heroin or nothin' like that – just 'like ta' smoke that shit, and kick that gong' and when there wasn't any, when the Chinese steward who smuggled it in got busted, wow! Could they hit the Jim Beam and the wine! Just like that, their whole lifestyle wiped out . . . no dope. That's how vulnerable the longhairs have become. While North Beach was gray and wicked, grass was scarce unless you had connections, and most of the people who later jumped out of that cocoon didn't have enough spit to wet a nickel. Pot will be legal soon, so you'd better save your seeds!

The next-best thing to do was read and go to parties and kick the curb on street corners and wait to see if maybe Ezra Pound might walk by, not knowing he was locked up in a sanitarium in Tuscany.

He'll be here any day now.

I'll see Kerouac if I wait around, or maybe Ginsberg.

Well, golly! You can go see Ferlinghetti any time, counting his sacks of money next to the 'I Am the Door Wall' in his basement!

No, I'll wait for Ginsberg. He's rarer.

North Beach wasn't like Old Town or MacDougal Street, or Berkeley, or anyplace. North Beach was all filled in with sailing ships and old Barbary Coast brothels and Pal Joey and Maiden Lane. Sailors tattooed and pigtail Chinatown, and hippies and gamblers and the fat belly of the Gold Rush bones picked clean by Collis Huntington and H. S. Crocker.

Now it's plastic, hi-camp, full-out-lust paradise. Lots of whores and Mafia and topless; but in the early sixties it was boring and dark, frighteningly sparse, a dearth of possibilities, a hopeless vacuum, a fear of earthquake, and some manufactured good times.

North Beach had a great jazz scene, and after all the tourists retired for the evening, some people would head for Vesuvio's, Coffee Dan's, or Jimbo's.

Jimbo's Bop City was a cave for evening crawlers who kept lookin' for a reason to stay up past any god-decent hour. Every freak from high and low hung out there in some kind of ghetto euphoria. It was an after-hours, setup place. Lambert, Hendricks, and Annie Ross would come out after a gig and head for Jimbo's first off. And Jimbo, who was a real guy, looked kind of like he was on stilts and would stand at the door to be sure all the celebrities got treated.

Some afternoons, Jimbo could be seen patrolling the 'MO,' as the Fillmore was called, in his white Caddy. Large red letters on the side of his car: JIMBO'S BOP CITY. He got a lot of mileage out of that ship and found a lot of boss stuff that way.

There were other bistros:

Vesuvio's was a hole-in-the-wall saloooon next to Ferlinghetti's store. Henri, the owner, wore his beret and smoked a pipe, authentic down to the black sweater and woven French sandals. You couldn't act up much in there as it was small, and if you lost your seat, someone, maybe a tourist, would flow right on into it. Displacement similar to Archimedes' principle, which was the slogan of the Gold Rush:

Eureka! I've found it!

Found what?

Eureka Street.

Anyway, it was a real *gemütlichkeit* place. Henri collected things and let artists exhibit there. But Vesuvio's was without jazz! The musicians were the big trip. Charlie Parker stories around then. Oral traditions even then.

BAGS GROOVE
ROUND MIDNIGHT
I REMEMBER CLIFFORD

Beat minds seemed to flex with that rhythm. Listened close to the jazz musicians at the BLACKHAWK because they were probably stoned. Catchin' a glimpse of Miles smoking a very fat joint at the JAZZ WORKSHOP. Big painting on the brick backdrop and Pony Poindexter's head and Art Tatum's ass and Fats Waller's pinky ring.

Life then was simple . . . phylogenetic recapitulations underground Be-Bop on a lower plane . . . it was the same gambling, scoundrel, whore-hustlin', musicianship, WEST COAST JAZZ! A big smooth MJQ tap root stickin' right down into the San Andreas fault of San Francisco . . . ground . . . earth . . . zero! That's the hum, hum de ho, of the whole thing. The whole fucking number was jazz and rock music and R&B and Bluegrass melted together, developing one step further.

Don Pedro Colley stands six feet three inches, in his sneakers. He is black like an Ethiopian – tall, lean-headed, a giant. He weighs about 250 pounds but can spin on a dime as if activated by some internal gyro device. Actually, he has nothing to do with the Grateful Dead – or rock music, for that matter – although he can be seen on television in rather large roles. In the saga of the North Beach turn-on, Pedro's role is much more subtle.

It never occurred to Odduck that Pedro would be hungry. Pedro was doing acting bits and going to a private drama class at the Fire House Repertory Company, a converted abandoned fire station, around Christmastime 1964. Lots of people used the facilities, and there were many activities there: There were political meetings, drama classes, a dance class, and small plays; in addition, certain rock groups occasionally used the Fire House for rehearsals. The floor of the large room was resurfaced hardwood, and mirrors and leg bars had been installed along the sides, as if it were a ballet academy. This large room was upstairs in the loft and was originally the firemen's dormitory. There was a brass fire pole in the west corner. One of the groups that rehearsed there was called the Great Society, with Grace and Darby Slick. They played for parties and occasionally in coffee houses in those days, and someone was throwing a bash the next weekend, so the Great Society was rehearsing at the Fire House.

The same day, Odduck had to visit a friend at Children's Hospital, on California Street, about three blocks away from the Fire House. After his visit to the hospital, he was going to meet Pedro and a guy named Sprang, who was a kind of neolithic genius, lost among all of these mods. Sprang was playwright at night, and a house painter in the daytime. You see, Don Pedro and Sprang and Odduck and another couple, who were caretakers for the Fire House Theatre, used to hang out there in the afternoons. It was a big, almost haunted, spacious place, and Sacramento Street outside was quiet. They had the run of the whole building, and they could slide down the fire pole to the garage and look as some of the artifacts of the pre-Earthquake days.

Anyway, Odduck is leaving Children's Hospital and he pushes the elevator button to go down, but instead of the elevator opening up in front it opens up in back, and Odduck finds himself in the sub-basement of the kitchen. But there's a door to the outside, so Odduck steps out onto the concrete floor, and the elevator door slides shut, whoosh! There's an eerie quiet in this kitchen; all the activity seems to be coming from miles of tunnel-like corridors in the distances; stainless-steel table moves by! 'What the heck is that, a turkey?' Yes, the smell is right; it's hot; lift the cheesecloth. 'BY GOD, IT *IS* A TURKEY!!!!! About twenty-five pounds, I'd say.' Is this turkey there for you? Was the elevator fatalistic? Probably set out here for me to pick up, sez Odduck to himself, so he picks it up, pan and all, and puts it in the broad-daylight trunk of the '48 Chevrolet, Fleetwood, Two-Door, with the Vacuum Shift, and nobody sees him – nobody even suspects, except the patients, who wondered why they didn't get any turkey. Ten minutes later, Odduck keeps his appointment with Pedro and Sprang and the rest, and he walks into this rehearsal this group, the Great Society, is having, with this steaming hot turkey in his arms, and guess what? Everybody in the building – janitors, amateur actors, dope dealers and musicians – all drop everything they are doing and go to devour this turkey. First off, Pedro grabs a drumstick, about three pounds, and splits to a corner. Then the others. Knives appeared from pockets; quickly, a sheet was ripped up for napkins; beer – where the hell did the beer come from? Hi-Ho crackers, kipper snacks. God! It's a feast! An actual frugal repast – like a Picasso etching, a flash of the Potato Eaters, Communism in action, ten people, hungry, got fed, by the grace of God. Christmas turkey gone in twenty minutes – bare bones, stuffing, everything. Cats ate the remnant carcass on the back steps and the band started to play. It was a bacchanal in the early afternoon. Strange, too, at around Christmastime, everybody starts to get sad – but not these belchstroms. It was getting dark outside. Practice room decorated with toyon berries (robins hallucinate on toyon berries from Marin County), and the band started playing a tune about a chick who took dope, and Pedro leans over to Odduck and says, 'That's the White Rabbit Song. They'll never get that played on THE RADIO!'

From the get-go, the hip people had to conspire together; strangers soon found the talent pool. In the whole city there was a very select and small, actual group of benzedrine night-hustler poets; all waiting to be discovered by the great talent scouts in the sky. But they somehow never realized that Ferlinghetti was the head talent scout, that he had a stable from way back, and saw to it that 'his boys' got the gigs . . . sort of a mafia technique . . . standard for an Italian from North Beach. The fix was on, and it seemed you had to be gay to travel. It's cured now. The rock and roll poets cured it . . . got to the buggers and scared 'em into irrelevance. Still, not all were queer – a bit mad, but not queer. The people that later formed the rock groups, like Janis Joplin and the Dead, had that yoke to carry. In addition to abject poverty, the young crazies had to carve out a niche in the marble-hard San Francisco Bohemian tradition. Well, some went to school out at S.F. State, or to City College, or to Cal Berkeley; some had straight jobs – Mike Ferguson worked as a coat salesman at Foreman &

Clark; Phil was a mailman; Page Browning (Dez Perado) worked in restaurants; others just kept getting higher and higher on whatever they could find. Out of the ethers, they drew their Quadrivium – numerology, Kazantzakis, astrology, jazz, bluegrass, and collections of kitsch little artifacts.

The kids started filtering in down from the country – Salinas or Oregon . . . afraid of the City, but come to dig, filled with subtle hatred passed on from Johnny Reb to 'Oakie' and finally to these south-migrating stump-booters attempting to decode bus transfers and blacks and street fights.

So the City-disenfranchised types met the country bumpkins. Two trains on the same track in the middle of the San Francisco fog. But instead of derailing, they augmented, merged and caressed each other. They became bedfellows – not comfortable bedfellows, but good-time bedfellows.

The nice, sweet, square and innocent folkniks met the sarcastic, urbane jazz worms, and North Beach spawned some kind of milt, some fertile juice, perhaps a cosmic seed dropped from a mother ship, or a twinkle of fool's gold sprinkled by the hands of the Magi. It got under the skin, got inhaled, got shot up, got sniffed, and rolled and smoked, and dropped and filtered, and blended and ground through a tea strainer, and rattled in a shoebox. Took trips on churches and sat out at the airport, and watched 707s take off and wondered how many Gs the people had to experience and hung out a lot, and stayed up all night.

That was North Beach, the only place where there were just hustlers. Then, ummm, girls started dropping out. No more celibate misfit cats. Now! At last, there were some twitchin' little honeys down from the country – eyes, legs – some good smells for a change. Black tights and berets. The people were finally gettin' an underground together. Some joy was gathering, for a change. Insane and happy . . . all at once.

'61 had been a dry year in the City, and from '62 to '63, there was nothin' but parties – good, stoned parties. Rudy Webb and Peter Parsley from S.F. State would always bring their drums, and there'd be Big Jeffrey with the starnight eyes, from Point Five in Big Sur. He could outdrum almost everyone, and Peninsula freaks would show up and they'd all get stoned and drunk and sit on the back porches in Noe Valley and North Beach. Just wailin' on congas and pots and pans and beer cans and voices, and everybody would dance. The most rock and roll they heard was Bad Interregnum James Brown and The Lovin' Spoonful.

You see, no rock groups in San Franscico got it on before anybody else. It all happened out of the same small, secular bunch. If anyone gets the prize, it would be the Charlatans. Consider the original Charlatans playing in Virginia City in 1965 for six months at the Red Dog Saloon. Their sound was halfway between John Philip Sousa and complete tom-foolery.

Odduck tells it this way.

The last time I saw Mike Ferguson was in North Beach in 1962, dressed in leathers and whispering about Mexico and what a flash, and living with two chicks who dealt grass – Chloë and the other one. He loomed up to my 1948 Chevy Fleetwood and whispered: 'Peyote, man. It's peyote.' Held up a button and waved me on down Grant Avenue, eyes fixed on the wonders of Venus.

So two years later I finds him playing in the Charlatans in Virginia City, Nevada. There was the Red Dog, as rustic as hell with the Victorian bar, and if you wanted to trip out, you could go over to the Zen Mine (cave in the desert) and take some peyote. The Merry Pranksters got hip to the Charlatans, too. It all started fast. Bill Ham had his light show rigged to the joint, and later brought it down from Nevada to the Trips Festivals. The final synthesis, the vortex, the acid tests. The Music. Let's do it. Do what? I sez to myself. Do whatever! comes the reply.

THEY SHOT THE PRESIDENT, DIDN'T THEY?

They? Who they?

(*Nobody knows for sure. Who cares anyway?*)

Right!

FUCK IT!!!

Let's do it, man!

Let's do it!!

Living between Dylan records can be catastrophic.

Mr. Tambourine Man, Masters of War.

Hey, man, dig this! The Beatles are into acid!

NEWSPAPER MAN: Are you into the occult, particularly the I-Ching?

GARCIA: It's a kind of magic and it's also a very wise book. It has something to do with time. We throw the Ching every time something heavy is happening. We respect all the famous forms of magic. We take into account everything weird that's happening just because we have found it to be so. Everything. If it's in the form of wisdom, it's usually saying something right at you. It's a matter of being open and you have to dig why it's appropriate.

CUT TO NARRATOR OUTSIDE NORTH BEACH TOPLESS CLUB:

Recently I had occasion to make an infrequent visit to the Cafe Trieste in North Beach, where the opera buffs congregate, right there on the corner of Vallejo and Grant. It's been there for years. Espresso and bagels and weird Italian pastries, and the Florentine marble floor and the wooden benches and the old posters on the walls still the same as when Clisandra's was next door. Instead of the WIG SHOPPE. Cafe Trieste even weathered the storm back in

’63. By then Clisandra’s was called the HOT DOG PALACE, like Pittsburgh on a hot summer night, vacant and frightening, but La Trieste still went right ahead with the espresso and the opera on the jukebox. If it was a Mafia jukebox, then it was a far-out Mafia. Had all the best operas, mostly in Italian (hardly ever heard Wagner), on extended-play 45’s.

Some guys would go in there and pay three dollars in quarters just to hear the complete La Traviata. And in between quarters, the old Italian guys, who really were the insiders in the place, would fight, *en italien*, about the operas and who was good and who was bad and how Caruso could really break a glass, and that kind of stuff, while the beatniks hung out and pretended to be uninterested.

I meets Odduck in there on Sunday, and he’s with John Alioto and they’re discussing some poetry, something about proper articulation and about LSD and the chick that fell out of the window on Oak Street in 1963, who we knew because she was Ciel Swanson’s roommate and Ciel Swanson drove Tom Purvis up the wall and crazy and how it was Purvis who loaned Phil the guitar down in Palo Alto. We were gabbin’ about that kinda stuff . . . really nothin’ much . . . when Odduck tells us this fantastic story about how he saw Merlin in 1967 . . . and he sez he’s on his way to San Diego to give a lecture on bad trips to the San Diego Men’s Colony and he’s changing planes in LA, and he’s dressed up and has dark glasses on and he’s walkin’ down those long octopus corridors and he sees Merlin and Kreutzmann comin’ down the walkway as fast as possible, Merlin dressed in a black cape and they is both carrying a guitar case but from the way they is walking, hunched over, it seems overly heavy so they both have to carry it into the men’s room.

Odduck peeks in, without saying howdy, and he sees these two guys open the guitar case and pull out a medium-size bottle of nitrous oxide, which is screeching like a banshee teakettle, like metal stress, and the bottom of the blue tank is all frosted over with ice.

The thing weighs about 100 pounds, so Kreutzmann holds the tank while Merlin runs hot water over the iced-up part, and the screeching changes key slightly, but water is coming out all over the sink and runnin' under the door out into the corridor on the nice machine-laid terrazzo, and businessmen are runnin' in and out and some guy sitting in one of the booths got pissed off because his underpants got wet from the spillover, and other bewildered travelers were in there yellin' and jerkin' back and forth. So Merlin takes the bottle into a vacant booth and sticks it (still hissing slightly) in a toilet and locks the door and crawls out from underneath the booth and pulls down his felt black matador's cap and adjusts his black cape with the red lining and sez to all the people in the room:

> Don't be alarmed – we are going to get the authorities and we'll be right back.

Then him and Kreutzmann run like hell to catch the plane.

That incident got into the papers, but it was largely distorted by the time it was news to anybody.

In the fall of 1964, LSD hit San Francisco like a bomb. A semblance of true underground communities had emerged. The streets were no longer filled with individual marauders. North Beach, the beatnik ancestral home, had more or less been vacated, left to the Mafia and the junkies and the established mercantile heads like Avrum Rubenstein, the painter, and Peter Macarini, the jeweler, and the coffee house owners like Leo Reigler, now pretty much set up for the tourists hot off the Broadway titty tour. Lenny Bruce wanted to see the tour bus from the Purple Onion have an orgy with the bus from Finocchio's (the male impersonator review). What a sight! Out in the street, these tourists from Waukegan, ripping off their clothes and balling.

The underground spirit had shifted to the Haight-Ashbury* and to S.F. State College. Actually, the college was the real functional nexus; the Haight was a stomping ground, a sort of paradise, for the intellectuals to find cheap rent. And it was, of course, a rutting zone for the annual spring hard-on.

San Francisco has two springs: one in the usual place, and one in the late fall, called Indian Summer. From 1964 to

*Named after Mayor Haight around 1880.

1966 the Haight neighborhood was timeless. There was no New York Moloch to tell you to 'keep in line,' no canyons of steel and brick to intimidate you. Nope, just folks and Victorian promenades on Sunday afternoon, and, of course, the Park – the glorious unfucked-up Park. There was no random murder, no brain sag. The cops didn't even have bullet-proof vests.

Around 1870, a guy named John McLaren (who studied yoga and probably smoked weed with Luther Burbank in Santa Rosa) fervently felt that the City needed a park, perhaps to offset the gambling and whoring that was going down on the Barbary Coast, or perhaps to con city fathers into spending some of the graft money on the people. McLaren had a vision to turn a four-mile expanse of sand dune into a paradise. That's right, folks; after all is said and done, every tree, plant and blade of grass in Golden Gate Park was put down and nursed and prayed over.

McLaren had the sense to put the flavor of every ethnic group in the town, like the Japanese Tea Garden, developed with the help of another ancient hippie, Mr. Gump, who said:

Good taste costs no more!

That's what's inscribed on his tomb.

The Haight became the center of the new hip aesthetic and cheap rent. The underground that emerged in the spring of the Haight was certainly not the kind of organized movement that one would find in Amsterdam during the Second World War, or even in Paris during the Impressionist revolution. But it was common knowledge that the Haight became a Schwabing, a Montmartre, almost overnight, but not – no, definitely not – a Greenwich Village.

One of the great human keys to unlocking some of the riddles that surround the Haight rests with a cat named Rod Albin. Rodney Albin is a down-home country harpsichord genius whose dad always worried 'bout him getting along. But somehow he managed to struggle through the College of San Mateo with Phil and Odduck, although a little later in time, and trudged the San Jose trail up to and running with

Paul Foster at the Off-Stage, and also kicking with his own little band called the Liberty Hill Aristocrats, who had a weird dyke manageress who blew it in their ears and tried to package this bunch of hillbilly radicals into a Lou Gottlieb Limelighter's format. Her attempts, of course, flopped, and left Rod a bit uptight for something to do. He turned to doing something that was on the cuff at the time . . . namely, managing a condemned Page Street mansion, which soon became known simply as '1090,' all the while attending psychology classes at State.

There could be no other 1909 in the world. It was condemned for the funk coat it projected and it was (the City thought) a haunt for hobos, and maybe in the way of the freeway, which (thank God) never went up or down. Rod took over 1090 at the request of his uncle, and the place became a center for State College underground liaison.

From 1090 Page, it's fairly easy to catch the 'M' streetcar, which takes you indirectly out from Haight Street to State College. All you had to do was take the #10 Monterey to Forest Hills, walk past the pink Laguna Honda Hospital wall with the inscription: 'Larry and David are Dirty Neo-Platonists!' and go down the weird elevator with the high school kids on their way to Lincoln or Lowell.

After a short sardine-can streetcar ride, out past *STONESTOWN*, the upper-middle-class shipping center. there it was, the stucco box quasi bauhaus machine that turned out Big Brother and at least part of the Grateful Dead, and the first resurrection of Dada in America. *The Love Book*. The Poetry Center, the very first Experimental College, the first drug rescue service, the longest eventual campus shut-down in the history of these United States and, of course, good old Hayakawa. In addition, there were the Charlatans, the Sopwith Camel, the Family Dog, some of the first Trips Festivals, and Rock Scully.

Rock Scully grew up in Europe and wound up in San Francisco going to school studying German languages and freaking out a lot. He had a partner named Danny Rifkin, who, like Rod Albin, managed a boarding house in the Haight. The two of them and Odduck and Truman Jones and Gene Esterbough and Peter Parsley used to sneak pot into the basement of the art building and get high and drink Cribari white Port (Crybaby) between classes. It got more out in the open as time progressed, and at spring registration (1964) joints were passed down the reg. line. The circle was ever widening.

In the fall of 1965 Odduck boasted about the Warlocks, a rock group he was managing out of Palo Alto, and he was posting pictures taken by Herby Greene. Herb Greene was about eighteen at the time, his ego had just melted on his first acid trip. I saw him with his cheek pressed to a window-pane in a house on the corner of Belvedere and Parnassus, tears streaming down his face, waiting for the rain. Gene Esterbough and Herby Greene and Rock Scully and Danny got to be tight partners as time went on, and there was this other guy who was also in that little clique – a guy named Ken Kief; that's right, that's his real name. Ken was playing guru that year, so he turned everybody on to acid because he was a psychology major and dug Velikovsky and Zen. He later wound up at a leper colony with the Peace Corps in the Philippines. These guys were hot to do something; not just be serious, but to do something 'fantastic' . . . always fantastic, never serious or commonsensical. So what else but to trip out with the Warlocks from the Acid Tests. That's how Danny and Rock eventually became co-managers of the Grateful Dead. They hung around and looked 'fantastic.' They both dropped school because the Warlocks were more fun, and fantastic. Odduck went away . . . it was too fantastic.

There must have been something happening in New York, but it seemed like it was just Andy Warhol taking pictures of the Empire State Building, while the West Coast people were stuck in their dreamy little San Francisco ghetto, not paying much attention to the world outside.

Who would have thought that State College would ever nurture a bomb-throwing anarchist, or that John Alioto's father would be the mayor? John schooled at State in the summer and took acid in the winter, and wrote poetry, and studied under John Logan, who was on booze a lot. And the poets would read stuff to each other and invite Lord Buckley over for a reading in the Gallery; and Gary Snyder, hot off the Zen trail, would come in; and, of course, anthropologists from all over. Why did good ol'Jefferson 'Fuck' Poland go on a hunger strike and everybody let him starve of ennui outside the ROTC office in 1963? What changed it all? ROTA?

President got shot, and things got awful mean, and Acid was just around the corner for millions, and already lots of grass. But there just weren't many smokers until 1964, when for some unknown reason the pot population trebled.

State College had more than weird personages and sterile buildings: it had weird geography. It was laid out down a hill facing the sea, which ya' never could view 'cause it was along the fog belt.

Now it's anybody's guess who the real mastermind behind the Charlatans was. Was it Mike Ferguson, who had evolved a sense of humor that transcended the usual droll beatnik humor of the period, or was it George or someone else? George Hunter, no relation to Bob Hunter, would come out to State and sit around and freak out with Richie Olson, who had been kicked out of the State College Jazz Band for long hair and other indiscretions . . . and after awhile George would seem pretty obvious there at the table with some 1890 garb on and everybody else lookin' like students, and him with his front tooth missin'.

Mike tells the following parable, which sounds true, at least on the face of it:

> **We were living in that beautiful old mansion on Franklin Street in Pacific Heights and George had somehow wangled a contract out of Columbia. We would have been the first band to sign (I think things here would have turned out much different) anyway we all sat around the kitchen signing forms all night, I signed and Richie signed and Dan and Wilhelm, then George stands up and says, 'If they'll offer us $25,000 why don't we hold out for $100,000 each,' and I says to George, 'Cause we ain't that good, that's why!' Then George went off on one of his sensitive trips and we all just never signed the contracts, we couldn't just dump George, it had to be unanimous, so the Original Charlatans just never put out a record.**

On Wednesday nights the film department at State, which was very advanced, and never got any credit for turning out all kinds of freakish little filmmakers now in Hollywood, would show unbelievable foreign films, chosen by heavies from the art department like Seymore Locke and Alexander Nepote.

The two Kens, Kesey and Babbs, and Roy Seburn would show up and look as off-campus as anyone could look. They, all the concerted film buffs, would sit in the theater and group-freak with a rapport unusual to large audiences.

Ya' see, the North Beach denizens were mostly a hybrid stockpot of mediocrity-sick people who came to S.F. State expecting a simple cultural transmission (like what Mom and Dad were paying for), and in some cases snitching sandwiches from the snackbar to stay alive and getting instead a huge pile-driver, cheesecake culture. The squares turned on fast, and that's where the dope came in. Oh, yes! It sure was. The Jungian psychology majors were the first people on campus to locate and scream about acid . . . the only other people who had LSD were the whorehouse operators who still lived up in North Beach. Ironically, the psych majors got the underground IFIF, and the Mafia types got the little blue pills from Sandoz . . . the 25 mg. Dylysid.

Anyway, none of it went stale. Not a single drop. Acid was selling for $7 a dose in sugar cubes then, before Merlin, before Kesey's mad chemist, and even before the Batman caps, the clear caps with the wrinkle in the bottom, or the Bear Aspirin, or White Lightning or Purple Haze, or even STP and the last bits of Sunshine. By 1964 the price in S.F. had dropped to $2.50 for the white caps and almost nobody was burned until '66, when the idea spread to the suburbs and bad trips started.

In the two years between 1964 and 1966, the Haight was a paradise of sorts. There was a clean dope economy – not much smack, coke or speed. It was a pre-ghetto blue-collar neighborhood, with a traditional cross-section of humanity: sailors, Chinese, Filipino, Japanese, blacks, Spanish, Portuguese, and just up the hill around Twin Peaks, a bunch of Anglos who sported big mansions on Buena Vista Terrace.

Mikto St Johns was a young chick who professed to be a madam, who wanted to be a madam from the beginning of her days in North Beach. She lived upstairs off Grant Avenue and always had a couple of other chicks living with her. You couldn't hang out at her rather elaborate pad after 8:00 p.m., 'cause that's when the tricks came in. Bail bondsmen, attorneys, cops, and judges, and guys with whips. Mikto had 'em all coming around . . . it got so good and North Beach got so bad that around '66 she moved her digs to a big operation up on the south side of Twin Peaks. Her clientele got bigger and bigger, and she got rich. She took a lot of LSD and hung out over in Marin County with Alan Watts in Sausalito. But Mikto wasn't happy. She was really bright, and she knew her niche was a cut above your average housewife, and she knew she could get anything she wanted, which she promptly did. Now she runs a maid service for wealthy bachelors. She thought the Grateful Dead were squares, *and she always considered Merlin rather obnoxious, since she got all of her LSD direct from Sandoz*. Status trip, I guess. She's a legend, and some say she can be noticed at Christmastime wearing a nun's habit.

North Beach had died for a time, gone back to the tourists. The Haight/Ashbury was the working psychedelic capital of the Universe, and not because everybody stayed closed in their own cocoon: They crossed the racial and social barriers and promenaded on Sunday through the streets past Ching's Market and Maggie's Beauty Parlor down to the Park. The merchants were glad to see the new influx of money, the students were happy to find low rent, and Sutro's Baths was still going strong. Seven baths empty, but the sideshow was still there, and the ice rink, and the 5¢ miniature music boxes with the wooden people inside. Sutro even had one of the original 'Tucker Torpedoes' on display, which looked like a rocket sled. (Wonder where it is now?)

HAIGHT-ASHBURY

Tantric gurus worthy of the utmost confidence have asserted repeatedly that youth can be maintained throughout the normal lifespan. Their prescript is simple: eliminate the mental and physical acids that cause death and death elements. To rid oneself of rigid thinking one should meditate through tantric sadhana, rouse the cosmic energy coiled in the root chakra. This will release neuro-hormones into the gross body, reinvigorating the physical and mental powers. This also creates a mentality that is dissatisfied with the status quo.

– Tantra

Whatever one may think of San Francisco, everyone agrees the architecture is unbelievable, and the unbelievable mansion at Lot Number 1090 on Page Street was sort of the Haight/Ashbury underground city hall.

1090 Page was built long after the Golden Age of Adolph Sutro, but it was a huge Victorian house, which stood as a masterful tribute to former times. The floors were hardwood parquet, set in the most unusual patterns, but the rosewood-and-oak spiral staircase and balustrades were decayed as if a dampness had haunted the place. In the basement stood the gazebo-like bandstand, with the moonstone glass windows around it. The ballroom was large and had rooms off to the sides, and it is here that Janis Joplin and Peter Albin and James Gurley started Big Brother and the Holding Company.

Actually, Janis never lived at 1090 Page, but she was always hangin' out there with her friend George the Beast. Peter Albin lived in the attic and went to S.F. State for two or three semesters, and a magician lived in front – not Edmund the Weird, but another guy (Edmund had since blown himself through a wall in Pacific Heights); and to top it off, a strange oriental anthropologist named Mr Sito lived on the second floor.

Believe it or not, the Sexual Freedom League even got started at 1090. At one time in her career, Ina Saslow, the co-founder of the S.F.L., lived there. Not at the peak of weirdness, but in the after-weird. Her partner was Jefferson Poland, who got busted out at S.F. State for possession of an outfit and twelve vitamin B-12 jugs. He also sat in the book-store to demand the sale of contraceptives and jobs for women, and he got busted for grass a couple of times. He changed his name to Jefferson 'Fuck' Poland, which confirmed suspicions of his sanity. This was probably what attracted Ina to him. They got the idea to wade-in nude at Aquatic Park, right in front of the old Italians who play *bocce* ball. The nude-in didn't sit well with the gentlemen.

About the same time, in the summer of '65, the free beaches opened. Just south of San Francisco on the coast, a number of beaches were liberated and, if you had half a mind, you could go swimming in the buff. At first the beaches drew a lot of attention, but the head of the San Mateo Public Health was a sly devil and decided to bust the voyeurs causing the traffic jams and leave the nudes alone. This was the green light. After the beaches were liberated, sexual freedom sprang up throughout the Bay Area with the energy of a giant erection. It was a spiritual quest. Jeff and Ina are still around, but not as active, politically or orgiastically, as they once were. Political orgies must be exhausting.

Ten-Ninety was always that way – starting things. It never got busted or raided, even when the downstairs magician shot cats in the park with his .22-caliber magic wand, to sell to occult practitioners. Even when the chick fell down the stairwell. Must have had awful good karma, old 1090.

Rod Albin and Odduck finished college – probably because they were almost done anyway – but the younger people all dropped out and said Let's make music, or sell dope, or start a commune. Some died from it . . . their souls died; others thrived. The drop-out phenomenon of 1964 was a plague to the hearts of well-wishing parents and a boon to the vision quests of almost everyone under the age of thirty. A lot of freaking took place after the assassination, between

1963 and '65 – two very stoned and amnesiac years – but it was merely a transitional period, just like all periods are transitional to somebody.

It was due to the rigors of school and cultural amnesia that Odduck lost track of his old friends. He wondered occasionally as to Phil's whereabouts and welfare, yet had no contact or clue. Even though he was married to a chick worth maybe a million bucks, he was unhappy; the future looked bleak at best. Then one fine, foggy morning as he came across the park, a ray of hope filtered through in the form of the De Young Museum, which had just opened a show of Chinese eccentrics. CHINESE ECCENTRICS? Odduck sez to himself, Wow, I'd sure like to see what a Chinese eccentric was/is. So the Odduck, in his white suit (psychiatric technician) started up the steps to the museum, and there he sees Phil and Ruth Pahkala going in. They looked a little wiped out; Phil looked green and sick, and Ruth seemed paranoid, and it was obvious that they were high on somethin'. It was also obvious that Odduck wasn't, 'cause he was on his way to work at St. Mary's. But they saw the show together and got high together on the weird little paintings:

Sage Contemplating the Cliff (which was upside down)

They saw Fantastic Rock One
Fantastic Rock Two
Fantastic Pedestals for Fantastic Rocks

They saw wall hangings from the poetry of Li-Po.
They saw castles floating on cliffs floating in
the sky, and the sky was simply floating.

An hour later they walked out and knew that they too were eccentrics and that the whole of Chinese destiny filled a mere three rooms in a museum.

They went separate ways, but Odduck got the address and they kept track of each other.

Haight Street started to look nicer than upper Grant Avenue in 1963, and it looked even nicer by 1965. Topless joints and high rent and pressure from the opera buffs at

Cafe Trieste and the tourists forced the Beatniks over to the Haight or out to the County of Marin, or Big Sur.

The folk music scene was going strong in Berkeley and Palo Alto. Garcia was seriously toying with the idea of forming a rock band. Everybody was doing some form of boogie-woogie and gettin' high. But North Beach was gettin' sorta rank. The Kerouac romance had worn off and the Haight/Ashbury District, across town, had no organized crime.

NEWSPAPERMAN: Who are you guys?

GARCIA: Well, I just see us as a lot of good-time pirates. I'd like to apologize in advance to anybody who believes we're something really serious. The seriousness comes up as lightness and I think that's the way it should be. The important thing is that everybody be comfortable. Live what you have to live and be comfortable.

While the San Francisco State scene was getting under way, about February of 1963, Phil had moved over from Berkeley to live with Ruth and a guy named Dennis Crank on Fulton Street. And it was at Fulton Street that Phil and Ruth became temporary guinea pigs for fat Dennis, who turned out to be a very psychotic pseudo-chemist who liked to concoct new dope and shoot it into naive people. Everyone who knew Dennis now realizes that at least he was an evil cat, but he was powerful and would drive around with a big plastic bag full of various dope, which was rare in those days – and like so many in those days, he had a long line of jive.

Phil liked riding with Dennis in the green Jaguar. It was fast, and Crank drove it fast in the fog, up and down the Great Highway, past the zoo, across the bridges. But one afternoon in particular, Dennis had to make a run to a chemical factory out in San Bruno for some meth fixins. Who knows how the stuff came out in the long run? Sometimes brown, sometimes purple, sometimes white, but was it anything? Dennis didn't seem to care. I think it was Silert he was concocting that day . . . the memory drug taken like poison oak tonic . . . a few drips T.I.D.

'GUARANTEED TO INCREASE YOUR IQ 20% IN TWO WEEKS!' That was the boast! The Jag pulled up outside the little company, and as the engine subsided, it was immediately evident that four squad cars were coming in for the kill.

What ya' gonna do with this stuff, punk?

Go fuck yerself. (Dennis was the violent type.)

Question the blond-haired freak. Maybe he'll tell us something.

Gee, sir, I don't really wish any trouble. I'm just along for the ride. (Phil was known for his timidity.)

Yeah, I'll bet. We know yer gonna make dope with this stuff.

Not me, I'm a musician. See, my hands are clean and my fingers are too long to hold a flask. Really, officer, if you'll just remove these cuffs, I'm sure we can talk things over.

We're running a make on ya' now, and if yer wanted for anything even traffic tickets, we're gonna hold ya' and the D.A. can decide tomorrow.

The cop was a fat bully from San Carlos High School, a police narcotics sniper, no doubt. He sidled off, breathing rapidly.

Oh, boy, oh, boy! A drug bust! Right here in our
little suburb. I knew we'd get one sooner or later.
Oh, boy, oh, boy!

Somehow, the charges were dropped. The cop didn't get his rocks off.

Shortly after that incident, Odduck fell by Dennis' new pad, near Ocean Beach to turn Phil on to some of the LSD from New York – the first stuff. They took the acid, but as the vibes were too weird, went down to the sea. They walked from Judah Street to Taraval in about 45 seconds (that's how they knew they were high). It was in the days before LSD was scandalous.

Odduck walked out onto the sewer pipe in his Johnston and Murphy shoes to have a few delusions of grandeur, while Phil sat on the sand.

Hey, Phil, I wonder what would happen if I threw these seven LSD cubes into the ocean?

I don't know. Let's ask the I-Ching when we get back.

About an hour later they went back to Crank's bungalow. Odduck contented himself with playing parlor games, which got pretty heavy – digging four levels at once and seeing Dennis, who refused to take LSD ever, through myriad layers of facade. Ruth was also there, and you could pick up on how intelligent she was. She attracted a great deal of light to herself, and Odduck could sense how sick she was of Crank and the hold he had over her. Phil was writing electronic music at the time and wasn't even considering playing rock and roll, but he had an imagination. Phil was up in his loft. He just threw a change – the I-Ching.

What does the I-Ching say? What would happen if I threw the cubes into the sea?

Well, the I-Ching says: Tui . . . the Joyous Lake. The ocean would be a joyous lake.

Oh, yeah!

From that day on, any sanity would be attributable to the I-Ching . . . it works . . . like the Tarot, it works, if you're ready for it and open to it, if you dig magic. There were thousands of people in San Francisco and environs who had the pagan faith even in those early days. Garcia and Marmaduke and Dave Nelson and Hunter were jammin' down in Palo Alto. The rush on the street was happening; the summers of '64 and '65 were poor but happy for almost everyone. By 1966 the Reznor brothers, with some money from their father, a wealthy San Francisco contractor, formed a corporation and leased the old Haight Theater right on the corner of Haight and Waller. Bill Reznor was sick of San Francisco State and the funky little Du Bois Club activities and saw a possibility of turning capitalist fast. He and his older brother Hilel wanted it to be the showplace of the street. The fire marshal hassled 'em for permits. The new mayor, 'Benito,' was calling the flower children 'fascists' – can ya' believe that – in Mayor Alioto's distorted mind the peace-loving street people were the fascists? Freud called it *projection!*

Finally, by tough work and a little greed, the Reznors got it on with cameras, promotions, and a tape-recording studio, and a rather expensive dance floor. The grand opening of the theater was like an acid test, but groovier sans Kesey. Just Janis and Big Brother and the Dead, and some people from the Airplane, and Neal babbling incoherently something about Taos, New Mexico. Mellow! We thought we had it made. The *Haight-Ashbury Oracle*, later called the *San Francisco Oracle*, originally the *Love-Haight Ashbury Bush*, proclaimed the efficacy of the Straight Theater as a community hall. Every night something was happening. Marathon encounter sessions, followed by yoga omings, followed by movies of Aladdin's lamp and genies, and the next night a serpentine chanting session with a band like Mother Earth or Sons of Champlain in the background. The Straight got funky. Last time I checked, it had died a putrid Haight-Ashbury death – all the windows broken, Tokay bottles full of vinegar lying in the foyer. But while it was swingin' it was a people's theater. Maybe the Reznors hoped it would turn out that way, after all. Anyway, the whole Haight-Ashbury overdosed and eventually died of cocaine toxemia.

Summer of '66 had its bad minutes, too. A poetess named

Lenore Kandell got busted for writing poetry about a girl who dug her boyfriend a lot and liked to do things that most people consider generally pleasant to his body. She also dug talking about what he did to her. So, like Lenny Bruce, Lenore got busted for saying the vulgate for fellatio.

Again, the city fathers desired blood. They wanted to make an example of the vaguely defined group known as 'hippies.' It was an ugly, dull trial that took months – to no purpose. Lenore did some time; everybody spent a bunch of money.

All the square folk, all the model-A Americans, all the depression-prohibition Americans were uptight about the 'hippies.' Not so much because the Haight-Ashbury was wide open and going full blast, but because everybody was getting laid. Girls and boys were actually indulging their bodies. Young, fertile men were meeting young, fecund women, and for the first time nobody had to sneak behind the barn. It was like a Keltic maypole dance, and of course the clergy, which decided to intervene, were astonished. For the first time in this young generation, morals were ignored in public. Something had to be done! The powers that be demonstrated their powers by attacking Lenore Kandell, who was simply expressing in print what was going on in the life-environment she saw each day.

There is an irony to all of this. When Mayor Alioto took over, the town went wide open on pornography. As of this writing there are at least twenty theaters in San Francisco, and more in San Jose, Oakland and the Peninsula, that show hard-core stag films, and even occasionally live sex acts on stage.

The hippies weren't doing it professionally – there wasn't a whore on Haight Street in '65 and '66 – it was all free, and it was due to all of this balling that the *Oracle* and other media started to disseminate information about VD.

What goes around comes around.

This was the slogan and byword. The clinics were swamped. The Haight Clinic did little to prevent or treat the clap referring all cases to Dr Ellis D. Sox (they used to call him LSD Sox), who was the city health director at the time.

But the migrants didn't really arrive in San Francisco until after the 'Be-In' in January of 1967, until after the news media caught on and decided collectively to exploit the scene. The phonies didn't arrive until the summer of '67, the so-called 'Summer of Love,' but the real summers of love were to be had in '64, '65 and '66, when people were undetected and unparanoid and mostly 'cool' San Franciscans. Those summers and years were the resurrection of the old Bohemias of San Francisco's past . . . the gambling Barbary Coast, the Gold Rush, and the International Settlement.

Those were the pre-hippie summers, when hippie was a word equivalent to 'groupy.' One day was worth a lifetime of memories, when young and old Bohemians got together, when Alan Watts wrote about his acid trips in *The Joyous Cosmology* and Ale Ekstrom sang sea chanties with his ocarina. When the blacks from the Fillmore brought their drums to the Panhandle and blasted away all afternoon on Sundays . . . drums cutting through racial barriers, flute players, free grass.

There was a lot of bush around then, too, and a lot of music. The Warlocks (later the Grateful Dead) were playing free in the park every weekend. Just sort of go down to the park and play. Merlin would get a big flatbed truck and generator and they would play all afternoon, and maybe Sarah Garcia's little group called Anonymous Artists of America would play, too. And maybe another bunch would jam, and the food would go around and pot would pass around. In a crowd, the joint never came back to you, so you had to take a big toke and hold it and pass it on. Bigger and bigger joints were rolled, and the parties went on in the sun and under the all-seeing eye of John McLaren and his rhododendrons. Kesey's bunch would show up between acid tests and look at home in the eucalyptus-studded Panhandle.

The street people were aware that the revolution was not secular. It was a world movement of people and music and freedom to be free. It was a revolution without the fear of police reprisals, because the balances of nature and the metagenetic will of the people desired freedom. It was a naive assumption, but in that phase of the revolution the same thought was had all over the global village. The young people were emerging from the ooze of the mechanical world and developing a consciousness into and beyond electronics. Thus, the music followed the will of the people. All the visionaries yearned for the next stage of being, the next skin of evolution. Fear was great, but curiosity was far greater. Thus, Kesey's bus became known as

FURTHER.

The parties went on and on; the Trips Festivals went on and on; LSD was legal, and it was a giddy truth that the street folks had (at least temporarily) put one over on the Establishment.

Since 6 October 1966 (666), LSD has been illegal in California. It was already illegal in many other states. The California law reads as follows:

> **11901. It is a felony to sell or offer to sell the following restricted dangerous drugs:**
>
> **(a) 'Hypnotic drug,' including acetyluria derivatives, chloral, paraldehyde, sulfomethane derivatives, or any compounds or mixtures or preparations that may be used for producing hypnotic effects.**
>
> **(b) 'Amphetamine,' including methamphetamine, desoxyephedrine, or compounds or mixtures thereof.**
>
> **(c) 'Lysergic acid,' 'LSD' (lysergic acid and diethylamide) and 'DMT' (N-N-dimethyltryptamine), including their salts and derivatives, or any compounds, mixtures or preparations which are chemically identical with such substances.**

The day the laws prohibiting LSD went into effect, a very large demonstration cum party was held in San Francisco to protest their enactment. This was a peaceful protest (as peaceful as a protest can be with rock and roll accompaniment). The poet Lee Myersoff made an introductory statement:

Young artists, writers, poets, musicians, dancers, craftsmen, holy men, and lovers have been gathering together in the Haight-Ashbury community for the last three or four years to experiment with and explore both new and old forgotten forms and meanings of art ritual and life. At the same time, the political and social life of America has become barbarous, brutal, hypocritical, and divided by fear and racism. Now the freedom of expression has been threatened here in San Francisco at the center of a new emerging artistic and spiritual community. If a new concert of human relations is to be developed in this city, this state, this country, and this world, the freedom of expression of all artists and citizens must be protected and preserved. The Haight-Ashbury is only an active manifestation of a world-wide youth revolution that has been infused with a revelation of the spiritual unity of all men and women of all races here and everywhere on all planets in all solar systems of all galaxies in the universe.

This set the general mood. Next, Allen Cohen, founder of the *S.F. Oracle*, read the following manifesto between breaks in music and ecstatic dancing:

When in the flow of human events, it becomes necessary for the people to cease to recognize the obsolete social patterns which have isolated man from his consciousness and to create with the youthful energies of the world revolutionary communities of harmonious relations to which the two-billion-year-old life process entitles them, a decent respect to the opinions of mankind should declare the causes which impel them to this creation. We hold these experiences to be self-evident, that all is equal, that the creation endows us with certain inalienable rights, that among these are: the freedom of body, the pursuit of joy, and the expansion of consciousness, and that to secure these rights, we, the citizens of the earth, declare our love and compassion for all conflicting hate-carrying men and women of the earth.

We declare the identity of flesh and consciousness; all reason and law must respect and protect this holy identity.

Danny Rifkin danced madly with strange girls, and a bad overcast time was had by all. I think it even rained that day, but one girl was happy enough to sing this little song, which she said was for e. e. cummings:

Everything
is building
here
SUMMERspring day
and I wander
WONDER
looking for
a place to
sit . . . apart
so that I can
hear
the magnificent
mornbird
churprunging
in the
        trees
even though
I
can't see
            IT.

In another celebration, on Saturday, 14 January 1967, at least 25,000 people came together in a 'gathering of the tribes' for a human be-in. This was held on the Polo Grounds of Golden Gate Park. We were seeking a return of this once-voluptuous country, attempting to regain the forests and great herds by chanting mantras, the songs of the Hindu Buddhists, and by focusing on the magic center of energy that was forming there in the back yard of the Haight-Ashbury.

This meeting was a baptism, not a birthday party; it was a calm and peaceful approbation, a reaffirmation of the life style, a settling of the waters. There in a splendrous array, one could see fans, feathers, plumes and tufts; bells, chimes, incense, pennants, banners, flags and talismans; beaded charms, lettuce-and-tomato sandwiches, balloons, paradise flowers and animal robes, bamboo, fruits and baskets; folded hands, closed eyes, bright brows and smiles, stoned people; prayer cloth and shaman sticks, floating, dancing marijuana flags with peace symbols, and the smell of the divine herb wafting through the void vortex that we created.

Thousands eating of the free food provided by the increasing awareness of these times and cooked by The Diggers. Turkeys, homemade bread, pure touch of the wandering Jew in the free soup mit kreplach. Upon the stage the bands, the poets, the priests, Ginsberg, Gary Snyder, Roshi Suzuki, Leary, a partially functional sound system wiring laid up and paid for by Merlin, Quicksilver Messenger Service chanting Hashish Ha-Ha. The Hell's Angels guarding the generator just like they would do later at Altamont – generator fixed and spliced somehow.

The Dead played, and someone read from *The Egyptian Book of the Dead*, spreading sound on sound across the gathered tribes, and Leary says 'The only way out is in.' Maybe a little misleading today – Leary a little stoned. The paradox of seeing the white eye on the side of the Indian is too much. The white race that once destroyed all of the red man's buffalo is now saving himself from slaughter by the loving mob tribe of Indians, 25,000, who wander about on this green turf, this public field where on other afternoons the wealthy Pacific Heist barons disport themselves atop charging polo ponies.

Barefoot girls in priests' cloaks, tie-dyed madras, saris, and corduroy teen-age braves stripped to the waist, flexing muscles in a hot winter sun; folk singers charting mountain ranges in their imaginations; shamans and motorcycle cultists, lovers, voyeurs, mounted police and hippies, cowboys and Indians, children; blue-black-white ring-tails hanging either side of glances, Chinese masked drum beater, Hell and Damnation preacher with a bullhorn and electrified to the speakers on stage. 'Man isn't smart enough to guide himself,' he shouts. Eric the Viking reincarnate passed back through the archetypes carrying a medieval doom-of-darkness cross and a skullcap from the Walküre stumbles through Bergmanesque flagellants. Magic theater.

Newsmen and cameramen and infants all struggling together to understand the amorphic nature of the event, because everyone just showed up and said: 'Here we are – ha, ha, ha – here we are.' Lenny Bruce, grinning in an after-life. Some Merry Pranksters with girls on all arms. Jerry Rubin shouting a political message from the stage, pleading for bail and condemning the police: The soldiers in Vietnam are tired of fighting – it's been a long war. Another Lenny Bruce insight. Hosanna from the crowd. Adolescent princess wearing an Indian headdress of orange, and a cloud of gold-yellow incense geysers from the stage. Janis Joplin hugs the poster artist Mouse all afternoon, gets drunk on Southern Comfort, can't sing. Dizzy Gillespie wanders off in the crowd playing his horn to the melody of coincidence, while the Jefferson Airplane plays some kind of rebuking mantra on stage. And from out of the sun, from what appears to be no airplane at all, a parachutist, much too small at first to be real, glides down toward us.

Looking up at the miraculous descent, we shout:

Pegasus!

Daedalus!

Buck Mulligan!

NO, NO, Icarus – he's going up!

Could this be the mode of transportation, the chariot of the gods, just a prank landing somewhere near Dick Gregory, stoned and Rolling Thunder, discussing the bail for Puget Sound Indians with Marlon Brando as a precursor to the takeover of Alcatraz?

Be-in goes on for hours.

The day is over, and the sun is set. Coalescing in the trees, thickening and converging onto itself. Bright day. No LSD rescues, and Alan Ginsberg said, 'Let's practice some kitchen yoga and clean up after ourselves.' There is a dispersal and refreshing non-showbiz attitude and reappraisal of the community. LSD was now illegal; we had to stick together – all of us, all types – and we had to clean up after ourselves.

Even though it was Poverty City, there were always good grunts around, and the newly relaxed and refurbished Grateful Dead moved into a house at 710 Ashbury Street.

Annie Corson was sort of the housekeeper and cook – wow! what a cook! – for the wastrel mob that lived at 710. The house got super funky, a sort of reversion to the Chateau days, only worse. The rooms were strung together, and everybody's stuff became everybody else's stuff. Hunter moved in, wrote songs with Garcia; Phil and his new girl Florence moved in – then out, then in – then out. Laird inhabited the basement. Merlin was often by, and the Hermit came in from the acid tests just over and still going on. It was a prankster house: The Dead had not started to break off from the prank, acid test melancholy goofing. Page Browning fell by, and Neal whizzed about a few times and broke the chandelier.

Going through the house was painfully like taking a Masonic Third Degree . . . 3°. Outside, it was lopsided, down-the-hill, slats kicked out, steps missing. It was painted, about forty years ago, a dull mustard color and was never repainted. The stained-glass window was nice, but even that had a crack in it.

The Grateful Dead office was unfunked for business purposes. Showbiz posters, somebody's makin-it-wallpaper, artifacts, illustrious Herbie Greene photos and a secretary named 'Henri' who was an angel, a sister of both colors, who kept the front room-office in balance while everybody freaked out upstairs.

Summer of '67 rolled by and the pogrom had begun. It was long feared. 710 got busted. Narcotics. Complete sellout of the media. Everybody sayin' 'Who's that? The Grateful Who?' 'Them actually busted! Oh, shit, Isaac, let's get out of here . . . Armageddon is just around the corner.'

Actually, what happened is the Hermit snitched everybody off, fingered 710 to save his own grungy neck and kept runnin'. Cops busted the house – Annie Corson wavin' to Jerry from the top window: GO BACK, MAN, IT'S A BUST! Garcia, like a reversed film, disappears. At 715 Ashbury, across the street, Laird and others just stood by dumbfounded. By now the band needed two houses.

Rock Scully and Danny Rifkin drew up a statement, and they called a press conference. Their statement is not infrequently heard in Bohemian quarters:

> **As you know by now, the San Francisco Police Department and State narcotics officers invaded this house on Tuesday for the unpeaceful purpose of arresting ten persons on charges of possession of marijuana. We have invited you back to our 'way-out pad,' as the *Chronicle* calls it, to discuss the meaning of this action. The arrests were made under a law that classified smoking marijuana with murder, rape, and armed robbery as a felony. Yet, almost anyone who has ever studied marijuana seriously and objectively has agreed that, physically and psychologically, marijuana is the least harmful chemical used for pleasure and life-enhancement. It is particularly less harmful than alcohol.**
>
> **But the law continues to treat marijuana smokers as felons. The president of a company that makes a defective automobile which may lead to thousands of deaths and injuries can face a maximum penalty of a minor fine. A person convicted of possession of marijuana can be sentenced to life imprisonment. The real danger to society, as well as to thousands of individuals, comes from a law that is so seriously out of touch with reality.**
>
> **The law creates a mythical danger and calls it a felony. The people who enforce the law use it almost exclusively against the individuals who threaten their ideas of the way people should look and act. The result is a series of lies and myths that prop each other up.**
>
> **Yet all we wish is to be free Americans – endowed with**

certain inalienable rights – among which, somebody once said, are life, liberty, and the pursuit of happiness. Is this so frightening?

The Grateful Dead are people engaged in constructive, creative effort in the musical field, and this house is where we work, as well as our residence. Because the police fear and misinterpret us, our effort is now interrupted as we deal with the consequences of a harassing arrest.

The police searched the place twice, found a very small amount of weed and, unfortunately for them, completely ignored the kilo that usually stood upright in Annie's kitchen pantry. That was escorted out by the *Oracle* people for safekeeping, which meant safe smoking. Only one thing to do: smoke the evidence.

Bob Weir got busted in that raid, which took place six months after he stopped smokin' dope and had gone into Zen macrobiotics. Weir was a man-child in the promised land – the only musician to go from rich kid to rock star, a really good-lookin', baby-faced rock star, a child, a monkey. At the acid tests he was climbing ladders and cursing at cops. I think he scared himself, and at 710 he couldn't resist the Ashbury water-balloon war, throwing all over, and into the middle pulls the cop and Weir could not resist and picks up a nice red one and cop's window is open. Nasty, nasty Bobby FIRES! Wet cops get mad, so Bobby got busted. One more strike for 710 Ashbury, ramshackled as it was and listing so terribly there in the rusty sunlight off Haight Street. Anyway, Weir quit all drugs for good, and ever since Janis OD'd, he has become a one-man army against heroin.

Bob Weir is, in Phil's mind, a new man, a homo sapiens novus, a man of the future. Perhaps Weir's insight about the horrors of drug use, especially heroin, was valid – but Weir could never see anything politically. The Haight-Ashbury experiment was doomed at its spontaneous inception. Because, from the very beginning of the movement, there were corrupting influences. Now, in every new social revolution there are corrupting influences, but not to recognize these tendencies (the petit bourgeois corruptions) is disastrous. The most obvious example of this co-option stands to this day as an institution called 'The Haight-Ashbury Clinic.'

The Haight Clinic is a 'free' clinic, but free in this context was never defined. Does this mean free to the patient – or free to the public? Does it mean that the spirit of the organization is free? Does it mean that the function of the clinic is to free the people? No; none of these. The definition of 'free' means that the doctor's time is not paid for by the patient, but the doctor's time at the Haight-Ashbury Clinic *is* paid for. There are innumerable nurses, doctors and dentists, social workers who are not compensated for their time. But, the Board of Directors of the Clinic receive large salaries – to say nothing of honorarium, book royalties, public appearance fees, remuneration from filmmakers, and large personal private donations, from grateful parents.

The Grateful Dead were approached on numerous occasions to do benefits for the Haight-Ashbury Clinic; but in each case, some odor, some strange essence exuded from the purveyors of the Haight-Ashbury Clinic's slightly unrighteous rap. One evening, Jason McGee, aged nine, accidentally took some LSD on Belvedere Street, and he freaked out and began crying for his mama, named Heddy, who was nowhere to be found. When Heddy was finally located, five hours later, she decided to take Jason to the Haight-Ashbury Clinic. But the Clinic could not detoxify Jason. They could only send him to General Hospital. Jason was taken to General Hospital, given a dose of thorazine and sent on his way. So – in addition to having large administrative salaries, the Haight-Ashbury Clinic offered little or no help. To this day, the Clinic hangs on – even though the Haight-Ashbury dream has been dead for years. And it is for this reason – and for rumors of other experiences – that the Grateful Dead are leery of doing benefits for rip-off artists and heart-beat social workers out to 'cure' the drug problem. Troll says: 'It's gonna take care of itself, anyway.' Either everybody OD'S or everybody grows up!

Drugs are an old phenomenon, and epidemics always chase after euphoriants. The Prohibition was an alcohol epidemic, and in medieval history there are numerous examples of ergot poisoning and LSD-like symptoms causing death from 'fitte,' also called St Anthony's Fire. The limbs actually rotted away as in leprosy. But if you think the present pot epidemic is weird, check out the 'mummy' epidemic of the 14th century. Unfortunately, the great interest in mummies and the money expended on their procurement were not directed to the acquisition of specimens for study and display, because by the time of the Renaissance, mummy had become a highly prized drug. In medical tradition, pissasphalt from the Near East had long been recognized as a curative drug. In trade, it usually was called *mummia.* Since the appearance of this natural pissasphalt was similar to that of the bituminous materials used by the ancient Egyptians in the mummification process, it became the practice to substitute the materials found in the bodies of the Egyptian mummies for the natural product. Abd Allatif, the Arabian historian and physician, writing in Cairo in 1203, remarks:

> **The mummy found in the hollows of corpses in Egypt differs but immaterially from the nature of mineral mummy; and where any difficulty arises in procuring the latter, may be substituted in its stead.**

The next step was to substitute the dried flesh of the mummy for the hardened bituminous deposits found in the cavities of the body.

Mummy, like heroin, was obviously a drug of considerable morbidity . . . it kills, but slowly. The soul first of all must go, then the brain tissues; then finally, because of the addiction, the will for life disappears and the body slumps to a walking coma, a Gogolian dead soul in a lock step. There was never any heroin around the Grateful Dead.

Compare the death drugs with the life drugs; compare the light to the darkness; compare the sound of coarse verbal speech to the wafting lyric of Dvorak . . . the way is clear to get beyond death: 'walk out of any doorway . . . feel yer way, feel yer way, like the day before.'

To look out of every window at 710 Ashbury would have

HERB GREENE

Garcia at the office.

ODDUCK

Joe Novakovich and his collapsible dog, Chateau front porch, 1962.

RAM ROD

Neal Cassady giving his Hamms lecture, 196
Note convertible in background—Neal was
working in a tire-recapping shop in Cupertin

Charles Ives

Bob Hunter (left), Jerry Garçia (center), and someone else? Greyhound Bus Terminal, 1961.

HERB GREENE

JOHN WINTER

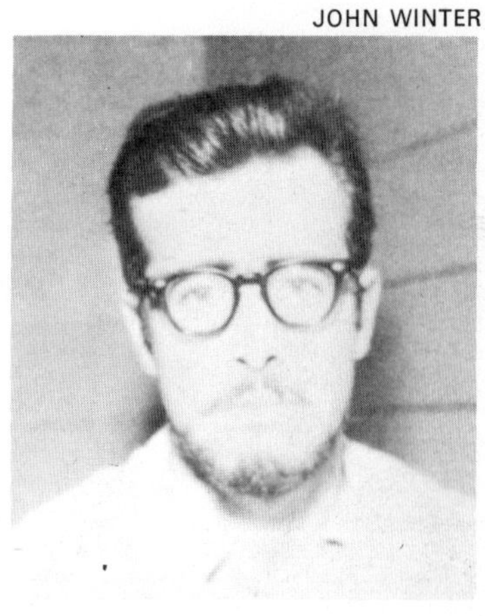

Bob Hunter at the Chateau, August 1962.

MIKE RACHOFF

Hell's Angels guarding us from nasty old man the day LSD was declared illegal, October 6, 1966. Golden Gate Park Panhandle.

BARON WOLMAN

Dead's News Conference. Scully's famous pursuit of happiness speech. Bob Matthews was arrested because he looked like Phil. 710 Ashbury Street, 1967. Left to right: Phil Lesh, Rock Scully, Danny Rifkin, Bobby Ace, Jerry Garcia.

MIKE RACHOFF

First Human Be-In, January 1967. Left to right: Gary Snyder, Michael McClure, unidentified man, Allen Ginsberg, unidentified woman, Lee Myersoff.

GIRL FREIBERG

David Freiberg (later of Quicksilve and Michaella, folk duet, 1963.

AVID GAHR

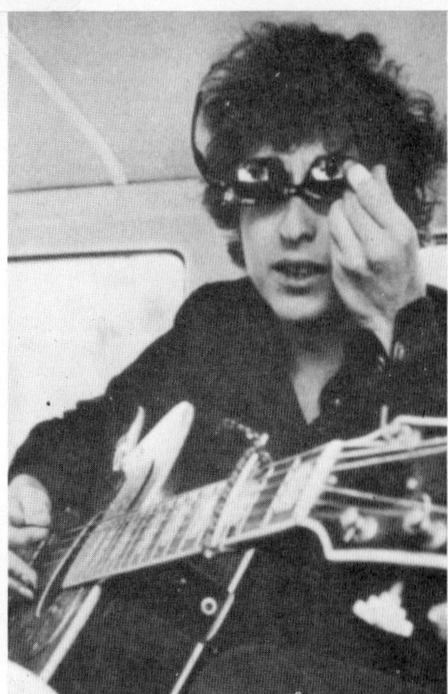

DAVID GAHR

JOE NOVAKOVICH

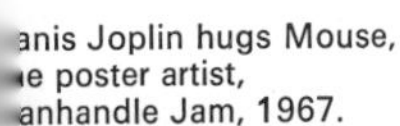

anis Joplin hugs Mouse,
e poster artist,
anhandle Jam, 1967.

See no evil, hear no evil, smoke no evil. Phil Lesh, Lee Adams, and John "The Cool" Winter.

RON RACKOW

PERMISSION GORDON WASSON

Chinese sage contemplating Ling-chi, the divine mushroom.

R. CRUMB

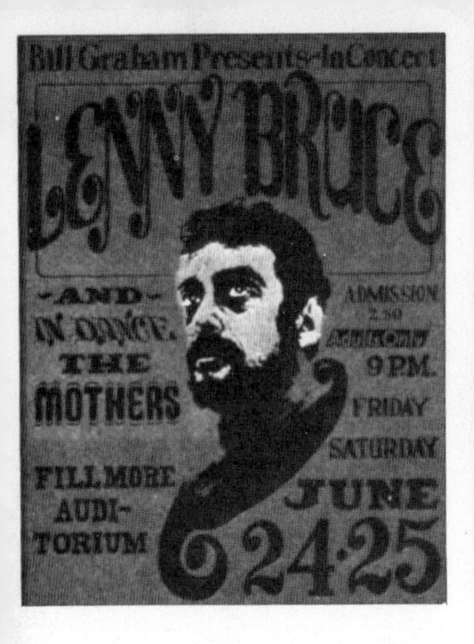

GET STONED!

Here's How!

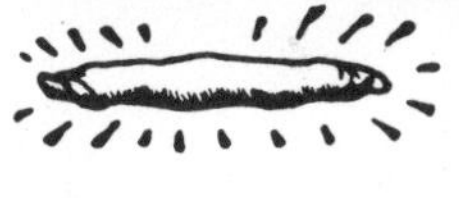

A Modern Miracle!

SMOKE AT LEAST TWO OF THESE EVERY DAY FOR ONE YEAR! THIS METHOD CAN'T FAIL!!

GET STONED!

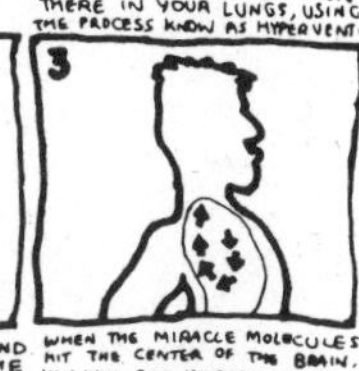

R. CRUMB

been difficult. Some were blind and led nowhere; others were psychedelicized and some were too dirty. Still, 710 was the house everybody chose to live in. Danny Rifkin managed it as an apartment commune for awhile. The place belonged to R. Crumb's mother. The cartoonist lived in the basement and rented the upstairs to the Grateful Dead, and later Bryan Rohan rented a room for his law practice called 'HALO' – Haight-Ashbury Law Office. Finally Crumb couldn't take it anymore and went off to create 'Mr Natural.'

In spring of 1967, Phil moved out of 710 for peace of mind, and he and Bill Kreutzmann found a place up on Twin Peaks. Bill had a girl friend named Sue who called herself Sisila. Phil moved Florence in, and that was a nice, cozy place, even though the rent was high. It was on the same block as the old church that Rohan bought and rented to La Val Benford.

But La Val was wanted by the Feds for something, especially after the LSD thing became illegal, and especially since Kesey was on the run and everybody was looking for the big bus, and especially since La Val had a similar bus parked out in front of the church. And especially because La Val is a black man. It was Paranoid City for awhile, so La Val split for nobody knows where.

Meanwhile, Phil and Kreutzmann are starting to lay a few coats of hashish smoke on their new apartment house walls, with the help of the Airplane people and Merlin and whoever else would drop in before the fall of '67.

Bob Weir moved in because it got too weird for him at 710 and he couldn't get his macrobiotic thing going with all the meat-eaters. Even Odduck came up from Santa Cruz and Big Sur to stay a week, and Neal was in and out, reading newspapers on speed.

Florence made good cinnamon coffee, and the landlord lived upstairs and never said a word and collected the rent. The Grateful Dead were in demand everywhere and they were playing a lot, maybe four nights a week. The band was moving in exotic musical directions, and Billy was a little slow here and there. He found himself a new drum teacher . . . a jockey-sized guy named Mickey Hart, a horse trainer, a drummer who had a drum clinic and school with Joe Morello – and an amateur hypnotist.

Mickey hypnotized Bill to drum harder and practice long hours by beating rhythms on a towel-wrapped book or a rubber drum pad – all done by post-hypnotic suggestion. Bill did improve greatly – so much that he asked Mickey to jam with the band at the Carousel. After that, Mickey joined the group permanently. He was the first new guy in the band – the first non-Californian. Where Bill was a drummer, Mickey was a percussionist. He spent a lot of time on gongs and cymbals, while Bill always sat at the traps and drummed the rock and roll licks. Mickey was a madman, a fresh breeze, somebody who was good, who was a pro, who hadn't taken acid yet, and who was a fountain of energy.

> **I was just thinking of nice words like Sergeant Pepper and Lonely Hearts Club, and they came together for no reason . . . They're a bit of a brass band in a way, but also a rock band because they've got the San Francisco thing.**
>
> **– Paul McCartney**

One night, shortly after the Sergeant Pepper Album died out and everybody in San Francisco realized the Beatles had been listening to their music, in fact ripping-it-off, Mickey hypnotized Bill as a parlor trick for Odduck and Phil and Florence. Everyone was just sitting around smoking these big bazookas of Panama red, and this beautiful crystal opium sprinkled over 'em and watching International Hotel on TV.

CUT TO SHOT OF W. C. FIELDS SMOKING OPIUM PIPE, DRESSED AS MANDARIN, ORNATE MANDARIN, WALKING IN FRONT OF MAGIC LANTERN RADIO TELEPHOTO MACHINE THAT GIVES THE VIEWERS OMNISCIENCE TO VIEW ANYTHING ON THE PLANET. CAB CALLOWAY FADES IN. SHOT OF CAB CALLOWAY IN WHITE TUXEDO (TAILS), WHITE TIE AND SHOES, AND FIFTEEN OTHER

MUSICIANS SIMILARLY CLAD, ALL JAZZED UP AND JUMPIN', PLAYIN' REEFER MAN:

Why does that guy walk that way?

Huh? Don't ya' know?
He is da Reefer Man
Why, man, he is high!

REEFER MAN, REEFER MAN
Boodoodiooodoo
I is da Reefer man!

Dreamed about a reefer
Five foot long
Mighty Mezz
But not too strong

Etc.

INTERCUT TO SHOT OF LIVING ROOM FULL OF HEADS ON BELVEDERE STREET. MICKEY SEZ:

Hey, all youse vipers, I'm gonna pull a little trick on Bill. I gonna make Bill think Odduck is Pig Pen. It's all done through suggestion. Watch!

Snap! One, Two, Three!

Bill goes into a trance.

Hi, Pig Pen!
Hi, Pig Pen!

Naw, Pig Pen never gets high, heeheehee.

Bill swears it was opium, but his drumming has improved immensely over the years. For months after the hypnosis sessions, Bill would go about perdiddling on books and rubber drum pads – everywhere just drumming away.

It was about the same time that Chocolate George, the bike bandit, went and died. The choppers could be heard roaring up Oak Street. Long lines, Gypsy Jokers and Angels and Satan's Slaves, in colors, bright, and helmets, and barbarous countenance, sadly playing out the death parade of Chocolate George. All the proto cops and various motorcycle poets like Mike McClure drove along with the processional. The Grateful Dead were honing up the scythe in the Panhandle. Another celebration. Chocolate George, the Digger, died. The bike freak's friend.

It was a fitting Angels funeral. Pig Pen cried a blues mass for Chocolate, and everybody felt the death vibe comin'. The press had got tired of hippie stories. *Newsweek* went away with all the color photos. 1968 was coming. Oh, shit. The hippies have died out. No more flower children. Now It's All Junkies. Every camera should have been smashed. It was a private party. The nation had no need to know. It wasn't news (the whole summer of '67 wasn't news), just the tribal gatherings of long-lost shamans. Now, of course, the beautiful dream is a slum.

And it was because of the slum that the second and final escape to Marin County is of great importance. It was another chance. Aside from getting things together, moving to Marin helped keep the Dead out of showbiz. They were the highest-paid unrecorded group in the world, getting $7,000 a night in some cases and turning some of that money into free gigs on Haight Street.

It might be said that the Grateful Dead rose to flame and misfortune by being the first and foremost haters of showbiz. They were almost the first of all the San Francisco bands to form and the last to cut a record, the last to sign a contract. Five contracts were turned down before they took the deal from Warner Brothers because Warners was the only company fool enough to let the Dead produce their own records from scratch.

The Airplane had bread from their first record. Not much, but some, and they were constantly restructuring personnel. They had two female singers, and a long list of drummers, Spencer Dryden being the best and longest lasting. Spence finally just quit from overduress and moved to Sausalito.

When the musicians moved to Marin County, the action moved too. And now, many years later, carloads of middle-class hair-swingers from Long Island pour into Marin every week seeking THE ACTION, and every high school kid has a guitar. The Dead had to move back into San Francisco after the first Olompali and Lagunitas experiences, but everybody vowed to come back to Marin to stay.

MARIN

Witchiti to
hiko wa
hora hito hora hito
he he he he
no wa

Water Spirits dancing round my head
Make me feel glad that I'm not
Dead
– Traditional Indian peyote chant

Sausalito was always a bohunk scene in the old days. It was a bohunk scene with the sailors and pirates and harbor captain smugglers who used to hang out there during Prohibition. The whole of Marin County was peppered with brothels and roadhouses out as far as Novato. Nero's place near the airforce base looks like a Mafia joint that might be described as early Bauhaus modern if it had been left to stand long enough. But the war came along, and the air-forced its way into the tranquillity of the cow culture there, and now the only exciting architecture is the huge Frank Lloyd Wright put-on (the only gaol he ever designed). It seems strapped to the hillside like a spaceship that serves layered toast sandwiches and club soda to the prisoners as if it were the ghost of the California Zephyr train steaming through the Royal Gorge at midnight.

Marin County is the current home of The Plant Earth rock and roll orchestra, but this fact will have to wait, because there were no rock stars on the scene in San Francisco in 1960 – only dope dealers and road men and gypsy troubadours like Kerouac's version of Neal Cassady, Jack Duloze, who seemed to be everywhere at the same time, uniting the various scenes into New Mexico out of Denver, and hanging around in Palo Alto at Perry Lane and Big Sur and New York with Pull-My-Daisy Ginsberg and in

Berkeley with some Hell's Angels. This was before tie-dye or macramé was a big symbolic thing. There was no competition – no fear of outside rip-offs. Merlin was still fiddling with knobs and dials and some classes at Berkeley's great university of the Golden Bear. Melinda was still whipping up dimethoxy molecules in undergraduate studies, with no knowledge of actual speed, for profit, just wisping about like a white witch in a lab coat among those pre-bomb campus creeks and trees.

Nobody really cared, and that made it all bearable. Nightwalking is the lonely joy that night people all hid behind, the perfect amnesia satori; psychiatrists call it 'mania erasmundus.'

In the nectared bitter pre-dawn streets that had blue police-light mosaics for windows. That was the tone of the time. Ideas about futures splitting rain-rippled puddles, while the feared paddywagon took all to jail equally, for one thing or another . . . at a time when vagrancy was still illegal.

Now, a shrink would say that they are/were all sociopathic amoral types. But why? Why, Dr. Shrink, did all of those sociopaths band together, a few in each town, and everybody running back and forth from place to place so that a grapevine was always scintillating? Is it not true of sociopaths that they are lone wolves, rarely seeking a herd? But they all did . . . a big giant family of

RICHLY }
Talented } Dopers
Brilliantly }
Immodest }

crooks and hobos, pimps and whores, bull dykes and burglars, jazz buffs and hip pervert junkies under-dressed fogwalkers who died of moonlight. Lester Young mentalities, all babbling the same insane Lord Buckley rap, the holy hipness, for once in the history the I with no I . . .

Instead, the ego was the whole Bay Region. Those times were wandering paisley hallucinatory fragments, and that's all anyone can recall.

Marin County was just a blanket of North Beach spinach and eggs from Dante's Pool Hall, waiting to get busted for barefootism, and pushing over to the Haight, and then pushing over to a sampan, sewer, Kowloon, opium, houseboats in the harbor of Sausalito . . . making it empty-headed across the Golden Gate Bridge to catch the action at the No-Name Bar.

In the acid test days, Neal Cassady started hanging around with the Grateful Dead. He didn't ever seem to have a home, like a pad with books and stuff. His home was the road, just like Kerouac said. A rail car or a La Salle sedan was his home. Somebody got his clothes washed for him, because he was always clean (in the summer he needed a clean T-shirt to flex his muscles in), but if he had a 'house,' nobody knew where it was. I quote a letter which reveals a lot about Neal's character:

Summer 1963

Harrison:

I am a MADMAN again? The old bug has done gone and bit me. The bug being Neal Cassady, or as you know him from Kerouac, DEAN MORIARITY (*On the Road*). This bastard is always messing with my head. He wants me to go to Mexico and then to the Guatemalan rain forest with him. I've got to get out of here before he makes me go.

Oh, I've gone on trips with him before; he's absolutely mad. I wish I could be Mad like him, but I couldn't stand the pain it must take to get there.

Neal came by today and really shocked (better word is amazed) my mother. We left my house and hopped into his old '49 Olds and took to the beach to hustle chicks. We smoked some grass on the way. The trip from my place to the beach usually takes twenty minutes; Neal made it in ten.

There were beautiful chicks everywhere, almost as if they were waiting for Neal. In less than thirty minutes Neal had picked out two young blondy types and with a wiggle of his finger the four of us were off to Monterey with a case of

beer and a bag of dope. The chicks flipped out and giggled and drank beer. Neal was doing about eighty through the Artichoke Capital of the World and carrying on two distinct conversations at once, opening beers with a spare hand and doing somethin' in the front seat that made his chick jump up and giggle and blush all at the same time.

Poor fucked-up me, I was having a time just watching Neal and hung up on the goes and does of life and caring a rat's ass (which Neal really didn't) and acting as a Superego and I couldn't have any fun except to see Neal as a truly free soul floating in the world of worried humans.

Oh, well, I give up. I'm gonna crash. It's 2:30 and I'm still at home with the folks.

Goodnight,

Joe

From this letter, you can see that all of the Bird stories (all the rusty 1950 hipster Charlie Parker stories) and all the Eldridge Cleaver growing-up stories must be rewritten to include Neal Cassady.

For instance, Neal was a bit of a con man, ya' see, and so he told Paul Foster always to check out the icebox first. If the people have a full icebox:

Then all ya' have ta do is ask people and they'll shell out. But . . . if ya' peek in the fridge and there ain't nothin' but a soggy Holland rusk and some withered parsley (and the light, of course), then don't ask 'em for nothin' and give 'em somethin' if you can!

In the fall of 1968, to mark the death of the Haight, Neal died for us. Pig Pen sang 'Midnight Hour.' Neal stretched out on the railroad tracks in the rain in Mexico and dug the sweet end. Kerouac wrote some blues and died soon after.

Neal always wanted to feel the tracks, wanted to get another FEEL of the Clickitty-Clack tracks. He wanted to feel the Iron and get next to it again. He was sad. One of his women invited him down to Mexico to the desert. But he never came back. There was an unverified rumor that he was pushed from a train by the Mexican Mafia, but that's doubtful.

Neal was a dynamo. You thought it was a crowd until it slowed down and it was only Neal. Up and down stairs, visiting at least one friend in each country town and city block. Who knows how many people dug him and didn't even know his name?

In a barbed-wire whorehouse in Winnemucca the chick said, 'You feel better?' Cassady always got the best treatment. Cassady was Hasan Sabbah's warrior. She said, 'Have another Burgie, Neal.' He babbled some more and went to sleep. She let him stay all night in Winnemucca, and that was his wife then and there, and his medical treatment for the week. Perhaps next week he'd find a lady to take care of him.

Ginsberg claims Kesey drained Neal's energy, and it's probably true; but Neal gave it freely. The Grateful Dead will continue to play for Neal and all of us. Stone Age circles still live, and the Druid will speak to Neal in Winnemucca, while Neal's ghost floats back to Cannery Row. So it all goes on. Neal died 'on the road.' He was tired of being a beatnik, a hippy, and a hobo all at once. Maybe it was because the hippies didn't recognize him and thought he was another shirtless drunk . . . as he babbled on the stage at the Straight Theater, holding a Burgie. But that rap isn't lost, either. The sound technician got it all on tape. Neal Cassady is immortal – a thousand times over. He was turbulent. He turned us on. He had a few wives strung out along the Coast, and one in Wyoming, I think, and one in Cupertino, who is writing a book about how often he masturbated. Babble . . . babble. Neal – legendary – died!!! 'Bird lives!' Right?

Cassady, following a Mexican wedding, staggered to the tracks, sand in the rocks; he propped his mouth open and drank a glass of pulque, one drop at a time. What purer thing? The voice came. The land is God, the land is Montezuma. There in the sky, Quetzalcoatl, flying saucer, long plumage, claiming Mother Neal Cassady. He even told Ram Rod he wasn't coming back from Mexico. Seconal.

There were a lot of guys influenced by Neal Cassady, good

or bad, bum or saint, and if you ever see two guys in the desert drinking wine and watching the sky eagles overhead, one could be Neal, and one could be, no doubt, Laird, who had the gross stink-foot contest with Novakovich in Las Trancos woods back in 1962 and had by 1967 changed his name to Barney: AKA: 'The Old Codger,' 'Oily-Paloily,' 'The Knight of the Golden Grommet' and the 'Van Master' – all esoteric monikers that defy explanation.

So by now maybe you've realized that Barney is one extraordinary fellow. He said he can do almost anything, but for sure he could fix the snakes of wirings at the acid tests, with a gas hose in his mouth and a chick humping on his left leg.

Barney was not really a Hell's Angel, although he had some original Levis that stood by themselves in the corner. No, actually Barney was a wiring man and a connector man, and a drinker's drinker and a piston driver, who just somehow grew away from the Haight and went to building houses. But Barney was impatient because he thought sure we would all die any day (impending doom paranoia), and he wanted to make it famous on his own before we all kicked off, so the Jack Daniels and the cocaine and STP helped him speed up and slow down simultaneously.

Barney (not able to believe in shrinks) decided he would do a far, farther-out thing: He shot some smack in one arm and some cocaine in the other, took about 500 micrograms of LSD and some speed and downed a bottle of some kind of hard booze (vodka, perhaps) and then some port wine. Then he waited until it turned his eyeballs around. With this mixture coursing through his circuits, he drove his chopper through the San Francisco fog and across the bridge to the Oakland Induction Center and got in line with the other guys. His leather-rivet Robinhood hat was glued miraculously to his head with Dixie Peach, and he was chawin' on some Copenhagen snootz or Beechnut or somethin' like it. Anyway, it always made him look like he was gonna spit in yer eye if ya' didn't smile at him just so. The desk sergeant yelled NEXT and up stepped Barney.

What's your real name, soldier?

I ain't no soldier yet, so just call me Barney.

Sez here your name's Grant, Laird. That right?

Yeah, that's right; was Laird long time ago.

What do you do for a living?

I'm a pimp; no shit, a real pimp!

Step into room nine.

Room nine contained a weird fag lieutenant psychiatrist who talked faggotry to the hard guys and there was Laird.

What do you do for a living, son?

I'm a pimp. I procure clients for girls that need money.

What causes you to sweat so much?

Let's see: vodka, cocaine, heroin, STP, nitrous oxide, Southern Comfort, pot and LSD.

Did you really take all that?

Yup, sure did.

How did you get down here?

Barney took the shrink over to the window and pointed to the Chopper being towed away by the Oakland police. 'Oh,' said the shrink, and Barney never heard another peep out of them.

Barney always ran around shouting CHRIST Jezzo Christo Mon! in the best Santa Clara Valley fifth-generation street Spanish. Ghrots! Chrits!

SUPER IMPOSITION
AND LAP DISSOLVE

FLASH BACK TO 1964 (PALO ALTO).

Barney is having a vision. See, there's Garcia lying out on a brocade sofa, fixing his stare somewhere through a stained-glass window, dreaming on a little bit of grass, having a vision: YES, YES, man. The Warlocks: a rock group! It's here. We can do it! He goes jumpin' up and down, racin' all around the High Street pad.

All right, we've got . . . let's see . . . Pig Pen play some blues harp and maybe organ, Weir play rhythm and Kreutzmann on drums, if I can drag him away from his job, and Dana Morgan can play bass, but he really don't wanna so I go Lesh, yeah, Phil, he can play it. Move down here with us, I'll have him playin' inna week! We'll do it like the Stones, throw in a little Dylan, maybe *Baby Blue* some folk rock. Yeah, we'll do it. We'll kill 'em!

The first American Rolling Stones concert tour comes around early 1965. It was a panic scene. The San Francisco Civic Auditorium was jammed with neo-dropouts of every style. The Charlatans were prowling about, some precursor Merry Pranksters, the Slick brothers and their little sister, Gracie, doing the Great Society number hot out of cellular Communism à la W. E. B. Du Bois Club and playing gigs at the Firehouse Repertory Company. San Francisco State scene goin' full blast, Danny Rifkin and Rock Scully flippin' out.

JUS
ABOU
EVIBODY
SHOW
UP
FER
DA
STONES!

The Civic Auditorium was packed to the rafters, people screamin' and stoned. (First time I ever saw a joint lit in public or a man wearing bright magenta lipstick for real. I think it was for real, anyway.) Everybody felt the multi-orgasmic reality of the time; it was one huge unison 'come' and for one holy-cosmic-transcendental second, it was all together. It was a benchmark for musicians who knew they were as good as the Rolling Stones. After the Stones' concert, Phil 'n Ruth sprung up to 1090 Page in Tom Purvis' Hillman Minx with the wobble steering, remembering Mick Jagger's lips swingin' around to *Satisfaction*, like slobber. Janis Joplin and some of the Charlatans jammin' in the basement ballroom, with Phil and Ruth standin' around and the Albin Brothers were there and David Freiberg and Gary Duncan were there, perhaps, to get the idea for Quicksilver Messenger Service, and Jerry Garcia was there and he sez to Phil:

Come on down next week; we've got a gig at a pizza joint called Magoo's!

Phil was kind of tired from fitting Jackson Pollack's Blue Poles jigsaw puzzle together and said, *Yeah, okay*, holding back his excitement.

Magoo's was stupendous, and things jelled quickly after the June of 1965. Odduck acted as manager for awhile and got the Warlocks their first club gig at the Fireside Club on El Camino Real – in San Mateo; but it was fraught with ID hassles. Weir was seventeen and looked fifteen, and the bartender didn't want him to be underage, so Odduck got him an ID from a notary or a fake draft card, or both. I forget. But the real hassle was trying to keep his mother from flippin' about it, 'cause she wanted Bob to finish school. But Bob was well on his way to being a bad guy, and there was no stoppin' him. It was Weir who told the Whole Earth Catalog:

If you want somethin' for nothin', jerk off!

He ran from high school to high school – all private, of course – and finally opted for the very progressive Pacific School, close to home, in the mountains above Atherton, near to La Honda on Skyline, where all the spinal trips and coded messages were carried.

All went well for Weir at Pacific; he was skinny then and they let him grow his hair long, kind of SUMMERHILL method, and he majored in music and chasin' girls. Bobby only got through one season at Pacific. His first report card gave him straight 'A's' in sociability, which when fully clarified meant pickin' and singin' and chasin' girls . . . the school thought it was cool. MOM thought it was the shits and Bobby was withdrawn.

He gained weight after many years of playin' in the band but never lost his ability to get into trouble. The following letter explains more fully (it was Weir who blew off a cap pistol – not a 'revolver'):

January 27, 1969

Mr Tom Sauce
Mojo-Workout Travel Agency
2143 University Avenue
Berkeley, California 94704

Dear Tom:

This will supplement our conversation of Friday, January 24, concerning the reservations for the Grateful Dead. As you know, our past experience with this group has been anything but successful. Briefly, they have caused so much confusion arriving at the airport with all their equipment just a few minutes before flight departure, shouting obscenities at our employees and passengers, drawn and fired a revolver (fortunately loaded only with blanks) at the check-in area and generally disturbed other passengers, that we decided to accept no future reservations for them.

After discussions with Mr Jack Dawson, our San Francisco Account Executive, who handles all entertainment groups, it was agreed we would accept this booking for the group – primarily because the Bill

Graham Organization is now handling them. Mr Dawson knows and has the utmost respect for Mr Graham's abilities in successful handling of other groups.

It is our understanding that Mr Sam Cutler will travel with the Grateful Dead as road manager. We would like to ask (as we do of all other groups) that on departure of Mr Cutler and the group (1) sound equipment, etc., which is to be shipped air freight be at the airport for processing 1½ hours prior to flight departure; (2) the group be at the departure gate for check-in one-half hour before flight time; (3) that enroute they conduct themselves in a manner that will not disturb other passengers on the flight.

I can sincerely assure you that we are interested in handling the air travel for all groups. *The one exception being the Grateful Dead.* Now because of the new management, we hope they, too, will enjoy traveling with us.

Very truly yours,

Dale W. Bauer
UNITED AIRLINES

The first really nice gig was at the 'In-Room' in Belmont, an underground hangout with wet bar but with enough money to pay about a grand a week, which was something in those days, when Charlie Mingus was gettin' $1100 for a week at the Jazz Workshop.

To the Warlocks, the In-Room was a haven. It was full of hard-swingin' middle-class airline stewardesses, hustling chicks, and slick-hair hat dudes who looked tough but dealt an inferior grade of dope. They loved the Warlocks, though. Crowds got bigger and bigger. The one-week contract worked into five and six weeks. The PA system blew out, but no matter. Things were good. They were actually paid under scale, and had to kick back some of the bread, but it was as much as any of them had seen in a long time.

After that, it was frustration mixed with joy. Autumn

Records was going strong. Their two big acts were the Beau Brummels and the Vejtables. The Warlocks were happy to be together and later went back to the In-Room with the Coasters, and there was old reliable Larry, the bartender, shoutin' and singin' and providing dramatic visual effects by filling the gutter on the bar with lighter fluid, and at peak moments during GLORIA, he would touch it off, and Wooooosh! Larry also used to take out his glass eye and make it glow green, somehow. It would just light up. Incandescent green eyeball, right there on the bar.

It was while the Warlocks were at the In-Room that Odduck got them up to the Matrix Club in the Marina to see a folk group with the hilarious name of JEFFERSON AIRPLANE. The Airplane were playing mostly acoustic instruments at the time, and the PA was an acoustically biased setup. The Warlocks, with all the amplitude, would have blown it out. The Matrix is presently closed but it may reopen. Who knows what can happen in the Rock and Roll universe? This little joynt was a major facet in the progress of the Grateful Dead and of the Rock scene in San Francisco. It was originally a daytime beer and pretzel place called the HONEYBUCKET, a hangout for police and stoolies, fringe gray world denizens and afternoon hookers. Its ironic transformation from 'underworld' to 'underground' was a true reflection of the revolutionary Middle Sixties in San Francisco.

Mat Katz, a balding forty-year-old entrepreneur, who had somehow designed a machine that puts plastic lids on coffee cans, put up some money for the club. Marty Balin, who was recently successful with a local group then called the 'Gateway Singers,' put up some more, and it's possible that Paul Kantner also had a hand in the original finance.

So, early in 1965, the small bistro called the *Matrix*, located at the foot of Fillmore Street – the Marina side of Fillmore Street – got started. It was nowhere near the ghetto part of Fillmore, but it should be explained that nowhere is very close to everywhere in San Francisco. The City measures 7½ by 7½ miles, and one-third of this is park land, Army turf, or uninhabitable commercial district. Eventually, about one million people get crammed into less space than Yokohama. With the addition of hills, San Francisco becomes a topologist's nightmare.

Anyway, Marty Balin, Mat Katz, Jorma Kaukonen, and Signe Anderson formed the first Jefferson Airplane, and they played in their own club. They also brought in much local talent: The Charlatans, Sopwith Camel, the Mystery Trend, Thirteenth Floor Elevator, and a group from Berkeley called The Fish (later known as Country Joe and the Fish). For really authentic blues they hired Blind Sonny Terry and Brownie McGhee, Barbara Dane and Lightnin' Hopkins. Eventually even the Warlocks played there.

The fact that the Airplane people had their own club set them on a rather firm financial base, but the Warlocks had to hustle for work.

Pierre's was one of the disasters in the struggle.

It was a topless joint on Broadway, and Odduck got the Warlocks in there to play behind the dancers, but the music was too good and the stage was too small. Down the street, Tom Donahue had a club called Mother's, with really psychedelic lighting and a far-out stage, but Donahue told the Warlocks to get 'a better education.' Too loud, too weird, or something. The place opened with the Lovin' Spoonful, and it was a colossal flop. Two weeks later, three employees were busted for anarchy and violent plans by being caught with bombs in the basement. Mother's became unpopular fast, worse than the curve at a stockmarket crash, from nothin' to less than nothin'.

Donahue went back to the record business, told the Warlocks to shove it again, and thought about a radio station. Stations with underground flavor are 'hep' this week. Anything that was 'hep' – that's where Biggy Daddy Tom Donahue was, always 'hep' and 'with it.' No matter what happened, lean or feast, Donahue always got fat, had foxy old ladies, drove around in big, downtown Cadillacs. Somehow every morning he'd stuff himself into a suit of sails and jam his visionless feet into some white gym socks and penny loafers, and get down to KYA office or maybe the recording studio to watch Sly Stone mix records.

The Warlocks got sick of this showbiz routine, sick of topless titty, sick of hopelessness. The sentiment was: If we're gonna make a million it ain't gonna be this way; they'll have our ass for sure. Meanwhile, the union had Odduck's ass for not having a license to manage or something, and the hills were waiting for everybody, so the Warlocks split, but stayed together. They decided to go up to Kesey's place in La Honda to see what was goin' on.

Merlin had by this time managed to supply Kesey's troops with dope(s). You see, to a dope dealer, Kesey was a succulent connection . . . nobody knows for sure how they met, so I won't bore you with made-up facts, but it was a very synchronous time. The Warlocks might have broken up for good if it hadn't been for Garcia and Phil goin' up to Kesey's place and hangin' out with Babbs and Kesey, and Stewart Brand and talkin' about a multimedia show. Then Babbs said, Why don't we do one? And that's how the Trips Festivals began . . . over in Soquel at Babbs' place right in the heart of rural Santa Cruz County. Pig and Bob Weir and Bill Kreutzmann showed up, and that was about all the music was – not rock and roll, just prankster music. Foster showed and Page Browning, and Hassler, and Mountain Girl, and Ron Boise, and the local freaks like Dick Smith the Dentist, and Peter Dema and Lee Quanstrum. The New Delhi River Band, consisting of Dave Torbert and Dave Nelson – and sometimes Marmaduke – showed up and later played gigs at 'The Barn' on the highway in Santa Cruz.

Merlin supplied the acid – clear Sandoz in red, wrinkled capsules. The invisible acid test, the speck and the wrinkle in the bottom. YAAAA!

Foxy Connie Bonner and faithful Sue Swanson showed up, probably because of Weir. The Warlocks used Sue Swanson's poolside back yard for practice sessions, but this drove the neighbors in Atherton mad. For the first time, everybody got stoned together at night, with Kesey and Babbs to oversee the project. For the first time the masks that were on the faces were painted on . . . the illusion was real, Sandoz saw to that. Paul Foster painted up like a purple-and-green Othello, lamenting his Desdemona. Babbs cavorted about in endless pranks and flippy mind boggles. Allen Ginsberg was there, and maybe one or two of his boys. It was all a blur. The bus waited outside with Roy Seburn to drive it. That was one bacchanal the chauffeur would not miss. The big bus was being painted more every day. Blue wheels, pink spots, the divan on the back flap, the portable generator maybe workin', maybe not. All stood outside for interminable hours waiting silently in the moonlight like it would just be abandoned by the celebrants, but it was fire. FURTHER was fired up again, and off they went over the hill very very very very very very stoned.

The midnight screeching second bardo joy hallucination kind of died down in the little hamlet of Soquel, only to be heard again in other out-of-town places, polishing the act up, tuning up the whole band for rock and roll music this time. Maybe even to turn on the WHOLE EARTH.

The next acid test was in San Jose on the night of the Rolling Stones concert, the second tour, and the door was kept by a cat called Big Nig, who very cordially set up a gig that made money for Big Nig and some to the musicians. That was one of the few acid tests that kept Kesey out of the money trough. The crowd was big and the guys in the band decided to put pressure on Kesey and Babbs to do a big production. The first human be-in was just around the corner.

Stewart Brand got the idea to hire the longshoreman's hall and maybe do a series of Trips Festivals, even at S.F. State, using Bill Ham's light show. The longshoreman's hall was big, and Count Basie had filled the joint three weeks before.

Somehow, Bill Graham got the deal set, and the Trips Festivals began, with the acid test scheduled as a small intramural event, not to be viewed to the exclusion of all of the other events.

The blue tanks of laughing gas were rigged with octopus hoses and with wiring, and somebody remembered to bring the balloons to fill. NITROUS-OXIDE TO TAKE OUT. Hoowhooo ha ha ha.

Infinite – it's infinite. The thunder machine donged, and closed-circuit TV showed Big Brother and the Holding Company with the new singer, Janis Joplin, and whooo – everybody stopped dead, even the freakish pranksters, and listened to the unearthly voice, the Gravel Gertie, Southern Comfort voice that Janis wanted to sing with as long as she could – nobody guessed how short it would be. Still, everyone wondered how long her throat could last.

Two weeks before, Chet Helms had split to Port Arthur to retrieve Janis, who had decided that home and Cajun was sweeter than North Beach and Beatnik. She was sick of the Fox and Hound, sick of Coffee and Confusion, sick of the Van Damme and Gate Six. At least Port Arthur had a cool breeze and clean-air-blues tradition, just about a half-day's hitch from New Orleans up the bayou. Johnny Winter was from there, and Taj Mahal, and Sun House, so Janis had some people to jam with, and other heavies we never heard of right there in the drillshack oil town.

Chet had to tell lies to get her to come back. The scene wasn't really ecstatic, but there was a lot of electricity around, and Janis fell for it like a quart of fried ice cream, started jammin' with Pete Albin and Jim Gurley. The acid test trips festivals sent everybody wild, looking for places to throw other gigs. Chet got the Avalon, and the Family Dog became known as a 'people's' rock and roll company, with the logo of Indian Joe saying:

May the baby Jesus open your
mind and shut your mouth!

Bill Graham got the old rhythm and blues Fillmore Auditorium, and the summer of '66 was down home.

Graham started having dances and concerts twice, then three times a week and for awhile he had something going every night. All kinds of combinations were tried. Musicians were hired and fired, and they hired and fired each other. Marty Balin and Paul Kantner of the Airplane were still trying to get rid of Mat Katz, left over from the Matrix.

Chet Helms was doing the Family Dog thing, too, and that was good, 'cause the bands were never mistreated by Chet, and maybe not by Graham, either, except by the sheer weight of his commitments to New York and the Burlesque Showbiz syndrome. But it was a merger for S.F. musicians and none of the bands considered the music scene showbiz, anyway . . . that was a value that had to stop in San Francisco – the old Variety value. The concept of the 'flash-act' was dead.

These people had class and were composers and folknix, not Fabian or Frankie Avalon or The Goofers or the Las Vegas lounge scene. These people were the true rustic underbelly of American music, the inheritors of some occult wisdom that came to rest in San Francisco. Also, it should be pointed out that the bands which started in San Francisco tended to stick together and take care of their own. The only show is the music. The Hollywood Hype is fading because of the conflict between Showbiz and San Francisco music. Showbiz is the old show-off music, the emphasis on entertainment . . . it's music with no brain and it's hardly serious music. It's background fill, mood music Muzak continually reinforcing that bullshit mediocrity that conditions the average listener's ear.

The Grateful Dead (nee Warlocks) wanted no part of that kind of music and didn't even think about commercialism in their trek through the period of the 'Great Society.' They became a non-identity halfway between the Warlocks, which was a pure linear rock and roll band and the acid test band which Kesey and Ken Babbs were trying desperately to solidify into something. But, the Babbs-Kesey thing-a-majig was fraught with all sorts of demigogic power games which the musicians couldn't understand . . . and which drained their collective resources.

In short when the acid test crust started to break off from the more elaborate Trips Festival concept the musicians started a non-systematic bifurcation of their own. A one-celled amoeba splits into two and those two into two *ad perpetuum.*

Everyone felt a new name was needed for the band. A full year had gone by since the first La Honda parties. Bob Weir suggested the Hobbits, which was what he was reading at the time. Kreutzmann suggested Vanilla Plumbego and there were thousands of other suggestions from friends and relations.

One afternoon Jerry and Phil were getting high at Phil's house in Palo Alto and they were hard at work on this new identity idea. Jerry and Phil felt the frustration more than the others and were more eager to focus and find a direction. Ruth Pahkala had an old 1912 dictionary that Garcia was looking through while Phil started pondering *Bartlett's Quotations*. There was a jolly sort of tension in the house that day almost as if finding a name was a do-or-die proposition.

Phil spouted a few obscurities from *Bartlett's* as Garcia turned through the dictionary I-Ching style. His eyes fell upon the words Grateful Dead, The. There was a long silence . . . 'What do you think of this one Phil . . . THE GRATEFUL DEAD! Phil fell off his seat in giddy rails of laughter; it had the right ring, something for everybody, an infinite array of associations Egyptian, Gothic, Mystic.

Garcia had stumbled upon a reference to the collected folk ballads of Francis Child . . . *Child's Ballads*. Child was an American scholar and collector of English and Scottish folk songs which he grouped into ten categories, such as *The Unquiet Grave*, *The Lost Lover*, and of course the one that caught Jerry's eye . . . *The Grateful Dead*. The ballads of the Grateful Dead are songs about ghosts who return from the grave to conduct unfinished business. If they are allowed to complete their duties they are grateful.

Ruth and Jerry and Phil ran over to the other house on Litton street. A toke of DMT first, before the presentation of the new name. There it was in black and gold letters scintillating in the Palo Alto Spanish sunlight:

GRATEFUL DEAD

'Sink your teeth into that identity, boys!' Thirty sets of dentures bit down on steel nails. 'It's a koan fit for an iron Buddha.' 'Grateful Dead' – 'How ridiculous!' 'We, the Grateful Dead, salute you!'

While the new identity worked a fresh magic, Garcia and Phil and Hunter and Pig Pen and Weir and Kreutzmann wanted to work on their music in a more or less unmolested, pastoral context. So a search was begun for a nice summer woodshed to get the family out from under the acid tests and trips festivals and other freaky phenomena. It's true, many events had an exciting air of historicity about them even while they were happening. Everybody knew it was a rare thing to have that much vibration emanating from that many people in the same place and all at once. An energy explosion, that's what it was, but tiring and exhausting. Just exactly how exhausting, no one knew for sure. There was an energy drain-off somewhere and the acid tests were still going on.

At the longshoreman's Trips Festivals, Laird Grant had acquired a handful of white lightning tablets from obvious sources and was going around popping 'em in everybody's mouth, especially his own. He went raving around amuck watching Bill Graham's renta cops play with slinkies and toy airplanes. Somebody dosed the renta cops, too, and Laird went around behind a cop shouting to everybody with a completely loco face, teeth seemingly filed to points:

Hey, looka that! The cops are high too.
Can ya believe that?
What d'ya think of dat?

Then the real heat came in, and Laird saved the day. He came on with the same rap, made the City police wait on the steps and then ran back inside and locked the glass doors. Just lock out the cops, that's all. Nobody gave a shit anyway. He blew a big raspberry their way and then melted into the crowd with his levis, grease glistening, and dangling the little fixit wrench off the belt buckle and poppin' white tabs like popcorn. I suspect he'll be very tired in the next two lifetimes.

The acid test started to be more of a dream than a lot of fun. Perhaps the highest and most exhausting Trips Festival was the Muir Beach acid test. That's where Merlin finally drove his car off the road and died. It was a death trip for everyone, but was Merlin dead or alive? He didn't know. He stumbled back to the beach, where the Pranksters were makin' whoopee, and the Dead were makin' snake music.

Merlin really believed he was reborn. It was a gray, overcast day, and the level was very stark. The waves crashed at maximum tide and the Northern California uniqueness started to burn its way in. Too much acid. Wind-swept cypress trees.

Phil was freaked out. He specializes in scaring himself, and he was looking for somebody to hold on to. Just at that moment, out of this crowd of souls, out of this seething humanity of small faces, one stood out. An olive complexion stared at him . . . coal-black eyes . . . perfect smile, reminiscent of the Da Vinci 'John the Baptist,' pointing upward to the secret place. That was Florence, as arabesque as the Firenze tile floors, as Gothic as the cathedral at Strasbourg. High on acid, Florence and Phil kind of got inside each other, and from then on Florence was a spirit dancing in films of scarves and making French hallucinations appear onstage as the boys in the band played farther and farther out. Somehow they survived.

For about a year after the Muir Beach acid test, the Dead played Dragon music – esoteric, asymmetrical music that could only be intellectualized by a few, and then most inaccurately. It was truly cliché-free, uncontrived music, even beyond the free-form jazz structures of Miles and Coltrane. When you're that far out, it doesn't matter whether you stop or keep exploring. You're lost in some sparkling divine oak grove, with only the glowing moon to smile down and say

FUDGE!

The acid tests were fertile ground, and the Grateful Dead, newly formed as they were, felt like new babies, and truly free. The equipment was a hassle. The 300-plus pieces of mechanique had to be torn down; Merlin's experimentation had to be carted off from place to place and repaired on the spot, and there were no manuals or trouble-shooting guides.

But a quiet genius known around the acid tests as Ramrod came down from Oregon with his pals Hagen and Jackson and Sonny Heard, and they just naturally started plugging things in and keeping track of Bob Matthews (Merlin's apprentice).

CUT TO SHOT OF MICKEY MOUSE AS SORCERER'S APPRENTICE COMMANDING BROOMS TO DO HIS BIDDING ON BALD MOUNTAIN.

Pragmatic guys from Oregon always work their asses off, drive all night, snort coke, gouge a chick a little, gross-out, dumb-out, and weird-out a lot, and don't care about convention or social amenities. Sometimes they're lonely, but they're old-fashioned and they stick to their ways. They are indispensable to the Grateful Dead. It's not just equipment. Ramrod passed the acid test; Ramrod was a Prankster; Ramrod used to look cockeyed on laughing gas and get really bombed out and still haul that equipment around. One night he had to escort Professor Lesh to his axe, so bombed was the latter gentleman; Ramrod had outdoped him.

One of the amazing ironies of the Trips Festivals was that a lot of the people who were there just didn't want to take the acid test. They didn't flunk it; they just didn't go get in line. In fact, when the Pranksters came out for their zaniness, certain numbers of the crowd would quietly disappear. Pig Pen was one of these.

Pig is supposed to have passed the acid test in a prior incarnation. For the time being, he was as high as he could get on Ripple or Bali-Hai or Silver Spur, or the vin du jour. In the real old days, he would smoke with the boys, but even that lost interest. No, Pig Pen just decided to market a package of himself just like Janis Joplin, and like Janis, that package included a high percentage of *spiritus fermenti*. Enough was enough. Pig had relentlessly resisted Merlin's coaxing and Phil's goading . . . '*What's a matter, ya' chicken?*' '*Nope, just sensible,*' *says Pig*. '*Saw some mighty mean beasts behind Jack Daniels. Don't want no scientific beasts runnin' 'round my head!*' Finally, somebody (the nameless are better left that way) got to him with a sealed beercan – the lip of which was liberally rubbed with, yup, L-S-D.

Pig didn't like it, had a terrible time, and felt like gettin' pissed off. But nobody did it to him again, until the last night of the Fillmore in 1971. Then, however, he liked it – said it made him feel 'transparent.'

Pig didn't like drugs to begin with, because in the Warlocks days there were many occasions when Pig was Ground Zero, wailin' and playin' harp and stayin' in key when Weir was so utterly spaced his head was nodding uncontrollably . . . not that he desired control. Bill was buzzin' on another orbit, too, different from Bob, and Phil was listening to the Edgar Varese in his head, and Garcia was soloin' right on through the intermission. That was the Trips Festival at S.F. State, perhaps the least popular and most analyzable Trips Festival.

Kesey was on the lam to Mexico, because he was busted smokin' dope with Mountain Girl, a minor, and him on probation for an earlier bust. But rumor had it he was supposed to turn up that night on the sheltered campus. Nobody ever saw him but some say he was there anyway, just like Errol Flynn, champion of justice and all-American boy. Kesey was there in spirit, but, in reality, he spent that night freezing his ass off in a boxcar in Guaymas.

After coming back up north from Los Angeles, the acid tests became public fast. Everybody got into the act, so it's obvious there had to be some 'family' parties, so there were these Olompali parties in 1966. Florence and Melinda had finally discovered a hippie country club in Novato, and the Dead decided to invite a bunch of 'the folks' for a housewarming.

Neal came and was a bit quiet and shy because it turned out to be a nudity scene, and Neal was, in actuality, modest. He liked to take off his shirt in public, but not his pants. Everyone had a little acid and the Dead played, and the bakers baked bread, and the people swam in the pool, and a Palo Alto photographer, Lee Adams, handed out movie cameras so that lots of people would be caught off-guard. Joe Novakovich and Neal arrived together and immediately found their way to the Merlin loft, which was the Patchouly capital of the world, and hit him up for some acid.

Got any acid, Merlin?

Nope, just what's in the dust on the bottom of the matchbox.

They looked inside. There was a thin corner of purple powder.

How much is that?

About 1000 micrograms. Split it!

Neal dipped in a finger and let the powder dissolve under his tongue. Novakovich needed a little more coaxing from Merlin, but he finally dosed up and they left. Joe had the uncanny suspicion that something had gone afoul, because his knees started to buckle on the way down the stairs from Merlin's room. And sure enough a whole day was hallucinated – pleasant, but completely unrelated to any standard holograph of reality.

Joe was rescued from the bottom of the pool. He thought he could hold his breath for an hour, and that's about the time the BBC arrived.

Odduck remembers driving his little Mercedes in and digging Curly-Headed Jim arriving at about the same time. They both spotted the BBC and noticed that they weren't taking their cameras and tape recorders from their Rolls-Royce. Unbelievable scene.

Here is this great historical afternoon
at the only hippie country club in the
world, and you guys aren't sure.

They saw the nudes, heard the loud music. They hadn't heard it before because it wasn't really their kind of music, and they freaked out. They were sucked back into their limousine and whisked away, looking at each other behind the pulled felt curtains and saying, 'I say, old man, so this is America!?'

Olompali reverted to a home for mentally retarded children in the winter, and the Dead found another woodshed in Lagunitas very near to the Quicksilver Messenger Service. And finally Olompali burned down, like 1090 Page, and Sutro's Baths. . . . The marks that some satanic power was in the wabe.

For financial reasons, it was apparent that the City had to be reckoned with. But the Grateful Dead unanimously decided to move back to Marin as soon and as permanently as possible.

CUT TO 1971 NEWSPAPER HEADLINE:

BAD TRIPS AT ROCK HALL –
REPORT OF SPIKED DRINKS

A concert at Winterland Saturday night recalled the early 'acid tests' of the drug culture, when containers of LSD-spiked Kool Aid were passed around at rock concerts.

About 1000 persons, most of them between 12 and 13, got unexpectedly stoned after drinking 'liquid refreshment' passed around at the Grateful Dead concert, according to police.

The concert, featuring the Dead, the New Riders of the Purple Sage, and R. J. Fox, drew about 8000 people, and Winterland was packed to capacity.

At the first intermission Saturday, an announcement was made from the stage. An unidentified voice said, 'Those of you who are going to get some liquid refreshment pass it on so your neighbor can have some.'

One girl said: 'It seemed like a friendly thing, but I flashed that anyone could put anything in it. When it was passed around it tasted like watered-down apple juice – I took a sip because I was very thirsty.

About forty-five minutes later, she realized an acid trip was coming on, and took another sip.

'*It was okay acid, but I feel sorry for anyone who took more than two sips.*'

'Pretty soon everybody really got going. It was like a church revival meeting.'

Bill Graham was unaware an announcement about 'liquid refreshments' had been made.

The point being that if you're a creative soul you don't need this kind of hassle to stimulate you. Acid tests, acid dosings, suicides, brain sag, over-rap and a bag-o-weed-a-day are energy drains.

The worst example of energy drain was Janis Joplin. She moved to Marin County – Larkspur, to be exact – about the same time as the Grateful Dead, but she was sucked into that weird East Coast exploitation scene that the West Coast 'hicks' have always been afraid of. In 1971, Albert Grossman purchased her psychedelic Porsche to place at the disposal of the various talents that he had working for him up there in Woodstock. 'See the death car on display, see the psychedelic car of the late Janis Joplin!' He has actually manufactured a small rural village to give the air of quietude to the recording studios he owns in that village; he has actually managed to convince people that a stage-set country is as good as the real God-made country . . . and that's what killed Janis. But most people know where her ghost is: It's down in the Big Sur with the rest of the hippies and Beatniks. . . . Down there with Jack London and Kerouac and Neal and Chocolate George and Dick Fariña.

BIG SUR

Carry a little 'tea' with you and you'll soon have an audience.

– From Big Sur and the Oranges of Hieronymus Bosch

Big Sur is intolerable!

Spring brings wilderness to Hurricane Point. Clouds come in late in the afternoon. Whales find their way mysteriously northward, and sadhus, musicians, Zen monks, and social workers all flock down that way. In 1961 it was intolerable because you could be absolutely alone. In 1971 it was intolerable because everyone had discovered Big Sur and you couldn't be alone no matter how far you got into the Los Padres Mountains. Henry Miller predicted this would happen.

Back about 1959, when they lived together in San Mateo, Troll took Phil down the south coast with marijuana stuck in his lungs, on a pilgrimage to Partington Ridge. Mailboxes on right side of road, unmarked ridge road on left side, about two miles south of Nepenthe. Climbed up the hill, and the two of 'em tried to find Miller's place. Failing that, the view was excellent. De Angelo's place was quiet – sunset, peacocks, stupendous. Phil flashed as hard as Garcia in the accident. The words from the book on star lore came floating through like a ticker tape:

The Chaldean figure of the dragon constellation Draco probably bore horns and claws like the Chinese dragons of a slightly later period, and probably had wings. The stars in the wings were eventually combined to form the lesser bear. Thus in ancient times Draco was much larger than the small bear; in fact, ursa minorus may have been expunged completely.

Did the Troll have a flash, too? Or was he even at that tender age cynical beyond help? There were times when he wrote advanced poetry and short stories that raised the hair on your neck and chest simultaneously. Then there were times when he rode around Sacramento with a Walther P-38, 9mm semiautomatic pistol on his lap.

CUT TO INTERIOR OF COURTROOM IN SANTA CRUZ. 1965.

The Troll was busted for having a beer and leaving his kid asleep in the car. He was searched and was found to have in his possession a small bouillon bottle full of a substance said to be Cannabis Sativa. Troll was a two-time loser. This bust meant that they had a special key waiting for him up in San Quentin, and they was only gonna use it once.

A courtroom battle ensued, at great expense to the Troll. Kesey's attorney, Paul Robertson, was called in. But somebody had to get him away from his jazz ensemble, called Wildflower, long enough to take Troll's case all the way to the Supreme Court if need be. The judge in Santa Cruz was flabbergasted at this approach. Case based on the idea that Troll meditates on weed and that marijuana is used, by him, as a sacrament. Religious freedom. The experts were called in. Joel Fort, the world's greatest expert witness, chemists, police, spiritual authorities, and finally the testimony of Father Shallert, from the Jesuit University of San Francisco. The Chardin capital of the omega sphere and the Roman Catholic Civic Center of San Francisco.

> **Yes, I think this man is a spiritual person and should be allowed to smoke marijuana in peace as part of his pursuit of spirituality.**

The Roman Catholic judge was about ta' blow his mind. Finally, after two years, the charges were dropped. Illegal search and seizure. Troll was free, but not acquitted – just let go, not famous for legalizing pot – just let go. That's why we feel the pain – the man giveth and the man taketh away. The Troll is very bitter nowadays.

In the early beginnings, Big Sur and the Santa Cruz coast turned people on much more than the North. Mendocino was too cold, too dreary. Maybe it was the stucco-bright, sunny resort town of Santa Cruz. Santa Cruz was the real gateway to the south coast – Monterey and Carmel were a bit slow in those days – still yawning away like a Steinbeck story. The Beatnik thing was going on in the City. Only the Jazz Festival was the big attraction to Monterey. The rest of the time we'd just pass on through to get to the Sur Country.

Bixbee Creek was the first stop after Carmel. Then, farther down, maybe even spend the night creeping up to San Simeon, down all the way past Lucia and Gorda and Lime Kiln, where about 5000 people had a wake for Neal in '68, sponsored by Vernon Gates from Palo Alto.

Vernon, on one exploration, said he found some longhairs from Los Angeles living in the wilderness behind San Simeon in some 14th century cupola brought back from Venice by Hearst. Contrasts were frightening in those days. The family built a fire and there was soot all over the tall Doric columns of brown-and-blood-red marble. The dome was open to the stars and carved in the frieze in Latin was:

Heaven above, earth below
Everything over under shall show
Joy to him who solves the rhyme.

The couple who lived inside this marble arch didn't dig the inscription or Vernon's intrusion . . . just another contradiction, another stumbling difficulty on the road to ego-mastery. By this time, people from all classes of society had 'dropped out.' The little ragamuffin family from Los Angeles didn't know the value of their marble house.

All ragamuffins vs. elitist arguments set aside, from 1960 to 1965 one thing was sure, one date stood out clearly in everyone's mind, one calendrical, sidereal date stood above all others as a mark of time: The Monterey Jazz Festival. It was a convention of everyone who cared and an autumnal rite. It was always held at the fall equinox, either by fate or feel, but not through the design of Ralph Gleason. Ralph somehow doesn't impress one as the autumnal type. No, rather it was some random divinity that swept down and made the KJAZ disc jockey, Jimmy Lyons, decide on that period. It was a rush to get the Monterey Fairgrounds prepared for 20,000 people (a lot for those days) and have the thing before the inclement offshore rains took out the profits. The Jazz Festival of 1961 was possibly the heaviest musical event of that period. Gerald Wilson's big band kept pumping out his *Blues for Yan-Ya* theme throughout the three days. Novakovich was drunk and crashing the gate, Garcia and Hunter and the Palo Alto crowd were there. John the Cool had taken to climbing flagpoles, monkey-style, and crowing at the cops that walked below with challenges to unseat him or pay the penalty. He seemed to want to announce something to the world, but he had nothing whatever to say except 'burp' or 'hurray for speed!' A picture appeared in the next issue of *Playboy* that showed a bunch of the people lying under a tree . . . drunk.

Odduck was hiding from the heat and his first wife at the time. Novakovich appeared and disappeared with the crowd from Emerson College which later became the Mime Troupe. Certain local celebrities stood out – Alvin Duskin and the Sandoyster contingent and the Big Sur hermits and a smattering of semi-underground disc jockeys and Kim Novak and other Hollywood types who hung out with Miles or Dizzy.

There wasn't much grass, but everyone was into those great narcotics – beer and wine and bread and cheese. You know – sandals, berets, bongos – the real stuff of the beat existence. Now and again somebody would come up with a green-and-white Dexamyl spansule or a bean, and one cat got sick behind some morning glory seeds (an unheard-of substance at that time). But it wasn't just the dope that was the get-off; it was the fact that the year opened and closed with the Jazz Festival, and for weeks everybody would get everything out of the way so he could get down there – hitchhike, drive, bus – anything. It was the real tribal gathering, later played up to the teeth at Woodstock. MJF was Woodstock for us, and the Newport Festival was a fizzle by comparison.

The Monterey Folk Festival was a later addition, and

colorless by comparison, mainly because all the blacks came to the Jazz Festival, while the Folk Festival was an Appalachian white bluegrass convention. Still, the spring Folk Festival served to turn on the local talents.

The blacks were the real thing, the early undergrounders couldn't get far away from the real gurus. They adopted, modified, and outright plagiarized the black lifestyle. They secretly, and even publicly, worshipped the black underground hero. No beatnik group is complete without its black influence.

Only in San Francisco, and to a smaller extent in the LA jazz scene, was the black man a 'full' and even leaderly component of the underground. What was once his entire province was invaded by the kids following Kerouac's trail. They were like innocent children playing in grammar school. Racial separation in the underground wasn't clear at all until the Muslims started preaching separatism. The beatniks would have none of it. The white Negro would defend his black brother, since the face didn't seem black. At Vesuvio's four black guys: JJ (Jimmy Johnson) and Carlos and Art Sheridan and George Pennywell all turned to Odduck and Mike Ferguson and said, 'Sure you ain't got some black blood somewhere?' Wow, man, they were passing for black! Too much! Ultimate compliment.

For Garcia and Novakovich and Willy and Hunter and the Chateau crowd, it was Lester Hellums or David X who played the black drums and talked the black talk. Troll went screaming barefoot down the side of Mt. Shasta: 'Yeah, we are beautiful, and so is the white Negro. Hurray for Norman Mailer and Lenny Bruce and Bob Gover and Lord Buckley – and all of them niggers and injuns.'

The jazz festival sort of died out after 1965. The musical ear had started to integrate black jazz with white jazz, and begun synthesizing Charles Ives with Gunter Schuller, had pioneered blues idioms into the symphony. And that was the start of the Planet Earth Rock and Roll Orchestra; i.e., EVERYBODY! Maybe at another time in future time, the orchestra will meet at the Planet Earth Symphony; maybe they'll be able to invite the KRELL from the Forbidden

Planet. Maybe soon it will be springtime sugar for music, and maybe in the toasty fall the brotherhood will strike that one and only note. In the meantime, when things get bad they can all make an exodus South to Big Sur. Even the first acid test was South.

Letter from Odduck dated Spring 1970:

By the spring of 1966, there were many indications that it was time to leave La Honda: The county officials had made it clear to Kesey that they wanted him to leave; his ever-increasing familiarity with the Hell's Angels was breeding some mutual contempt; the rains came even when the sun was shining a few miles down the canyon; and the plumbing was stopped up.

Hassler and Peter Dema opened The Hip Pocket bookstore in Santa Cruz, and Babbs had already left La Honda for the 11-acre ranch on Rodeo Gulch of Soquel early in 1965.

Hassler and Peter grew their hair long, much to the startlement of the other Pacific Avenue merchants, and embarked on a program of goofing that eventually led to the downfall of the store.

A lot of people have fond memories of the Hip Pocket. It was a good bookstore. But there seems to be a lot of misunderstanding about the function of the place. Many people seem to think that the main objective was to sell books and that therefore the store was not a success. Not so. The main objective was to have fun – and by this criterion it was enormously successful. Of course, Peter and Hassler did go broke and had to go elsewhere to continue their ravings. By the time they got done, a radio minister was saying that 'A sewer runs through the main street of Santa Cruz and that sewer is called the Hip Pocket Bookstore.' They got obscene phone calls by the dozen, and several art exhibits drew anonymous telephone complaints. After awhile they answered the phone: 'Dirty Book Store.'

I guess there were too many offensive things about the Hip Pocket. Ron Boise's statues, for one; the nudist magazines, for another. And the crazed, lecherous behavior never sat well with the city fathers.

Boise's gigantic statues of naked men and women were raised on the front of the store with great municipal fanfare. Various city officials were present and had the highest praise for the two enterprising young men who were establishing a cultural beachhead on Pacific Avenue. Only a few complaints were registered about the apparent nudity of the huge copper man and woman and the only serious complaint came from a lady whose residential apartment in the St George Hotel had its view of Pacific Avenue blocked by a huge, copper ass.

The nudist magazines kept the store on its feet during periods when books weren't selling like hotcakes. Most of the nudies were sold about 6:00 p.m., when all good families were just sitting down to dinner. The typical customer was a middle-aged man, rushing home to dinner, who would stop in to browse in the literary magazine section for a few minutes. Then, when the store was clear, the typical middle-aged man would grab one of the nudist magazines, rush to the cash register, plop down the exact change, and ask to have it secreted in a paper bag. One of the clerks, when confronted with this situation, would look to the rear of the store to see if anyone else were in the joint. When there was, this clerk would open the magazine after ringing up the sale, hold it up and shout loudly toward the rear: 'Hey, lookit the tits on this one.'

A display of photographs by Walter Chappell, who had been living among the New Mexico Indians, brought down the official fury of the community upon the heads of Peter and Hassler. They were busted for displaying obscene material, contributing to the delinquency of minors, and some other hokey charge. They were acquitted.

But by that time, the full Prankster crew had arrived in town and Hassler was losing interest in his book business.

Some of the Pranksters were at the 'Spread,' others had moved in with Bill Laudner in the old yellow house at Seventh Avenue and Soquel Road (recently torn down to make room for a self-service gas station).

Kesey had parked the bus at the Spread, and Boise's truck was there too. Joe Lazowski was beginning to let his hair grow a little and was starting to experiment with Day-Glo paints on Boise's thunder machine and other musical instruments.

In La Honda there were lots of Saturday night scenes to which were invited any and all who might want to watch a bunch of freaks in action. Filmmaker Kenneth Anger was invited. A chicken was disemboweled during the show, causing Anger and others to leave clutching their bellies. I think the unpleasantness of that particular Saturday night scene was another signal that the time had come to leave La Honda.

Anyway, Kesey and Babbs decided to continue the Saturday night stuff at the Spread. Babbs spent a lot of time hooking up one of his weird microphone-tape recorder systems and various rock bands played loud music. (This included the official acid test band, later known as the Grateful Dead.) One Saturday was unusually busy at the Hip Pocket Bookstore, although few books were sold. Neal Cassady brought Allen Ginsberg and Peter Orlovsky in on their way to the Spread. Several dozen other people stopped in for directions. Dema was getting a little uptight because of all the traffic through the store. At that point, I think, Peter wanted to sell books for a change.

One Saturday night I walked in to find a large number of persons standing around watching Kesey, Babbs, Mountain Girl, Ginsberg, Cassady, Orlovsky, Orlovsky's brother Lafcadio, and Pancho Pillow in the living room. Pancho Pillow, aptly named by Mountain Girl, was saying things like, 'Hey, there's a far-out trip I want to lay on you,' and the others were dealing with Pancho as men who don't

need trips laid on them are likely to do. After the Pancho Pillow scene ended there was music, freaking and . . . at one point someone, maybe Kesey, maybe Paul Foster, announced that this was the first acid test.

CAN YOU PASS THE ACID TEST?

NO LEFT TURN UNSTONED!

We all had to find out. In groups and singly we began moving frantically around the countryside setting up acid tests and Trips Festivals and pretty soon Peter, who didn't dig acid anyway, was the only one left to mind the store.

Santa Cruz remained the focus of the acid testers until they left for Los Angeles and Mexico. But things were changing at the Spread and at the old yellow house at Seventh and Soquel. Bill Laudner left to become equipment manager for Jefferson Airplane. Hassler left with the bus. But returned after a three-month journey that ended in Manzanillo with Kesey, dodging Federales.

Ron Boise went to Texas and came back. He wasn't feeling good and got drunk and talked about it. A few days later, he died. I remember 'Paint It Black' by Mick Jagger was on the radio when someone phoned to say that he was dead. I cried and later that night there was a wake for Boise at Paul Robertson's house in San Jose.

In the fall of 1966, the Grateful Dead family moved back to San Francisco, into 710 Ashbury, after the Olompali party. This Marin breathing spell acted as a much-needed rest and transition from the Watts acid tests.

With the exodus North, the Dead's group identity took on an even greater concreteness. The family was finally definable and in focus, and the mitosis from the acid tests and the insane DMT prank mentality was almost complete.

Annie and Jimmie Corson moved into 710 to take care of the kitchen. Mountain Girl and Jerry and Sunshine were building a little nest, Phil was getting serious about recording, and things had a more stable substrate. But as the stability increased, things got even crazier. Free gigs in the park on Sundays, with Saturday night gigs in Santa Barbara or Sonoma or at the Family Dog. The changes went down faster and faster, still no private space, still an urban commune, still no peace of mind, lots of fun but no peace of mind. A permanent move to Marin County seemed pretty important by the end of 1967.

Any recording contract seemed remote. The sound was good. Columbia wanted to get the boys into a studio saddle, but Columbia was turned down. 'Coumbia wants to dick with the mix all the time.'

A rich flamenco guitarist who was also a student at S.F. State (named Gene Esterbough) had a little studio on his Buena Vista Terrace mansion around the corner from Odduck, who had sold dope and struck it rich on the stockmarket.

Esterbough wanted to get recordings under way, so the five Grateful Dead cut a record on the Scorpion label called 'Don't Ease Me In,' which was released and died. Never more! The boys were already tired of the seven codeine postures and the perpetual Haight Street riots and wanted a rest, so it came time to move to separate houses. As an interstitial step toward fleeing the City altogether. Right in there somewhere, maybe the summer of 1966, the Dead signed a contract with Warner Brothers. Because Warner's Reprise was the only company interested in an open contract that allowed Jerry and Phil the freedom to mix what sounded good to them.

Joe Smith, the veep at Warner Brothers, tells it this way:

At the time I signed the Grateful Dead Contract, I was in any number of jobs. I think I was a singles A & R man, national promotion man. I came up and saw the Grateful Dead one night at an unforgettable evening at the Avalon. I'd never seen anything like that, never seen a light show, or people freaking out like that. That was in early 1966.

I was not at that point one of the two principals of the

company, I still worked for somebody, and I got a great deal of static about signing them, 'cause the deal was stiff, I gave them a fair deal, but I knew that our record company, if we do represent something of today's music, could not afford to let the Grateful Dead go, they are too much a part of the . . . and too much a fact of it, regardless of whether they meant a lot of profit for our company or a minor profit, they're too important for us to let them go somewhere else.

Well, that's the corporate viewpoint, but just to get it set once and for all, just to set the akasic records straight, there are no stars among the Grateful Dead, there is no leader, there is no big extra hide-bound ego maniac that jumps around on stage and inflicts his personality on everybody. There is hardly anybody more talented than anybody else within the band itself. Instead of megalomania, there exists a very fine sense of checks and balances and that's how the plow gets pulled.

In the early days, especially during the first records, Phil Lesh was the electronics mastermind, taping in on the extensive and precocious education he developed with Luciano Berio. Later, when Tom Constantin got out of the Air Force, they conspired to do even more electronics stuff, but by that time Garcia had developed his guitar technique beyond almost anybody in the industry, and he and Hunter had a little, possibly more beautiful, lyric conspiracy cooking. Thus, the balance was achieved and Tom, who had some adaptational problems and wanted everybody to be into Scientology, just gradually melted away.

On the surface it may seem that this checks-and-balances system is awkward and filled to the brim with calumny, but it's the age-old TAO workin' out; and besides, accidents happen; there ain't no better WAY. In ancient Egypt, musicians, like priests, actually died for their cause. Phil fortuitously discovered an album title in one of Churchward's Mu books.

In the early 1930s, Egyptologist Paul Schliemann discovered a tomb containing the remains of an entire orchestra. He writes:

We have been excavating the ruins of the ancient temple at Sais, in Egypt, for five months. Among many other interesting archaeological discoveries we have found a burial chamber of the musical celebrities of that era. Here in one of the catacombs, supposed to be from the time of the 3rd Dynasty, we found a huge casket of stone and with it a most unusual collection of musical instruments. It contained also a papyrus that has not been deciphered yet but I am of the opinion that *it is a peculiar kind of Egyptian musical writing unknown to us. The hieroglyphic inscription on the sarcophagus says that the musical instruments belonged to the orchestra of the Temple of Sais, and were used for the crowning celebration of Pharaoh Amen-emhat I. Among the instruments that we discovered, there were some that produced such sounds as, for instance, the roar of the wind, the waves, and songs of certain birds, and various mysterious voices of nature . . .*

Most of the instruments of an old Egyptian orchestra were of wood and porcelain. There is only one horn of brass-like metal. The strings of their harps proved to be made of a fiber absolutely unknown today. It is exceedingly thin and strong and has almost the appearance of silver wire. But then again there are strings which our chemical experts declare to have been spun from human hair. An orchestra of sixty-five instruments and a chorus of eighty singers were required to perform the majestic *Anthem of the Sun.* The instrument that seems to figure as the most important piece of the orchestra produces a hollow monotonous tone of haunting effect. The instrument is made out of a bleached human skull, the cavity of which has been made like an artificial throat of some supernatural monster. It is evident that this instrument produced a register of unmemorable sounds, but it required a musician who knew the secret of his instrument, therefore it played a unique role in the orchestra. An inscription on the small bone says that it contained not only the sounds of other instruments, but that also of the human voice. It was called the 'dead' throat. [Emphasis added]

EPILOGUE

What a long, strange trip it's been

– 'TRUCKIN' '
The Grateful Dead

When men are lonely and huddle as children
They mistake the prattle of fools
For the voice of the sage, so desperate
Is their search!

This was graffiti scratched on the wall of a Stanyan Street loo in the back of a funky donut shop across the sleazy street from Kezar Pavilion, where the roller derby rolls on and on, every year or so, and where Henry Thomas, the boxer from San Jose State, was eaten for lunch in the ring with chewing-tobacco stares and cockfight mustaches belonging to greasy gangsters of that 1960 era, when the '49ers stunk loudly and the Judah Streetcar clanked so close yet so far away from the man-made park, and Rod McKuen, ignoring all the pain, made up romantic, irrelevant songs.

Now that everyone has moved out of San Francisco, the City seems festooned with flies, a groaning, blind hippopotamus. At night she shines a bright smog-pink glow with sea-air intensity, streets slick with moaning weights too over-burdened. Laser red tits on bridges span the old small-town cow goddess, now a Gothic metropolis. Extincting death orbits heavy and close, and Satan Abraxas shows his face.

The City never had much of a slum.
Now it looks like

CLEVELAND!

Some people live in a Hell of their own choosing, but . . . we know Philip went pee-wee off Partington Ridge; we know Odduck saw timelessness; we know the Troll saw St John

Perce as Marpa melting snow in cavernous mountains; we know Crazy Horse rides on the wind; we know Garcia had burned brightly, falling through the air a thousand spans in that auto accident.

90 cubits
171 stadia . . .
Vision of the Roman Circus.
Divine
Mirth
of
Children . . .
TRAUMA!
SAMHADI!
What's
the
Difference –
Everyone still has to pray?

What happened in Palo Alto was the musical beginning of a cultural 'goodness' that can come from the lack of any addicting system. It was the completely unanimous decision to do away with 'style' altogether and still have the stuff stand as stuff. It was the search for total ingenuity, total breakthrough to the Tao, the naturally occurring system that is the galaxy, and beyond that the stellar universe, and beyond that the void blackness of infinity. It was within or without this system that the Grateful Dead agreed to compose or decompose music, write or paint or dance, or just simply sit and breathe clean air. And it is within this same system that the Grateful Dead urge the younger people to create

Quickly, quickly . . .
Before the earth flies to bits!

Paul Foster coined a byword that goes roughly:

Freak freely, 'cause the heavies will handle it when the time comes, but the heavies can't handle everything so clean up your own pad and keep your stash cool.

Well, there weren't any patriarchs in 1960, just a few saints scattered about here and there, and your usual assortment of junkies and eccentrics who don't fit the square hole. As a result, they all had to be super-responsible, and the weight was there, like a big electronic brick hanging in the future. They were hounds chasing nothing that they could ever catch for real:

If you chase a tiger you will
not catch him if you sit and wait
for him; he will not come to you!

Somehow they all took Zen seriously, and that saved them . . . from the what was to come, and since music is the purest art form, and is supposedly devoid of conscious meaning, and since pure music operates almost entirely at the unconscious level, to communicate the awareness of a family or a culture, it would seem natural that an extended family, such as the Grateful Dead, would seek to build a moral community consisting of persons who are primarily concerned with expanding awareness.

Among artists, scientists and technologists this increased awareness is so highly critical as to be a vital life force. The instant awareness decreases within the family, the greed trap starts to open; when the greed desire-urge is reduced or controlled, the feeling of increased awareness returns.

It is the dream and hope of the Grateful Dead that small moral communities continue to grow. These families represent the true nature of all future people who are presently subjugated by the paid-off and unaware community – which is obviously massive by proportion.

CUT TO THE GRATEFUL DEAD ENTOURAGE, INCLUDING *THE NEW RIDERS OF THE PURPLE SAGE*, LEAVING THE AIRPORT IN CHICAGO IN 1972.

'Hey, Garcia, did ya' see the Altamont Movie?'

I've only seen bits and pieces of the Altamont movie. The rest of the guys have seen it, and they didn't dig it. I didn't

want to see it, really. It's like doin' a song about violence – amplifying and promoting those vibes. I think that anyone who's puttin' anything out into the media, into the mass consciousness, has got a responsibility to try and put out good things, positive trips rather than negative trips.

I've been in a position to experience that phenomenon. Ever since we put out 'Casey Jones,' on Workingman's Dead, ten people come up to me every day and want to score some cocaine. If anything it's an anti-coke song.

GETTING ON THE PLANE:

I like to avoid that thing in every respect. I've only learned through error, because I've been an idiot on a certain level. Say that the movie was a good movie, and that the photography and the editing and the whole way it was put together was beautiful, and even the stop-phase murder was ballet motion, a dance of death. In spite of that, the people who'll see the movie are not all going to have the ability to view that thing on an aesthetic level, or to absorb the impact. It's puttin' down one more paranoid possibility, one of the infinity of paranoid possibilities. I think Altamont was a valuable experience for everyone who was able to learn from it, and I think that everyone who was supposed to did. I don't think it's for everybody. I don't think *anything* is for everybody.

That's what we hoped. Obviously, it was something very heavy for us to see what we had initiated by just, on a good day back in '65, goin' to the Panhandle and settin' up and playin' for free – we saw it turn into *that*. I mean, it wasn't lost on us, man. Altamont was the price that everybody paid for having that little bit of sadism to color their sexual scene. The Rolling Stones put out that little bit of leather. Obviously, there's a lot more to it than that, but I prefer this view. It's because the environment I live in is a high-energy one, and everyone is really conscious of this shift – we've all had that experience, of saying the wrong thing (or the right thing, as the case may be) and all of a sudden . . . bam, it's a whole different situation.

PLANE TAKES OFF.

I've worked out the essence of the way it was that day, and it was so *weird*, man. I took some STP, and you just don't know . . . Phil and I, we got off the helicopter and we came down through the crowd, and it was just like Dante's Inferno . . . the River Styx. It was spreading out in concentric waves. It was weird . . . fuck, it was weird. It wasn't just the Angels. There were weird kinds of psychic violence happening around the edges that didn't have anything to do with physical shit, I don't know – spiritual panic or something. And then there were all those anonymous, border-line, violent street types, that aren't necessarily heads – they may take dope, but that doesn't mean they're heads – and there was a lot of, you know, the top forty world . . . pop tarts, and anybody could have been a killer, or everybody, for that matter.

GARCIA FALLS ASLEEP.

So, we say this prayer:

No more: Altamonts,
Lenny Harts
Hell's Angels
Junk Yards..........................No more slip-ups
from helicopters
no more sleeping
rock stars
irresponsible
dope dealers
fuck ups

Next time the site must
be correct. But light and happy
not heavy and stupid and wind blister.

No peyote/heroin endless
Chelsea Hotel nightmare anguish
bullshit.

OK?

Let's shake on it!

The Grateful Dead may be the fashion one day and a bunch of losers the next. They do a song called 'The Loser,' which hits on this very theme. But they're not trying to win anything, so how can they lose? They're not really in the rock and roll game. They just play music. Bill Graham, he's in the rock and roll game. A reporter once asked Bill Kreutzmann to describe Bill Graham, and he said, 'Cro-Magnon, but through some miracle of television Bill has mellowed out.' In the early days of the San Francisco struggle, he was a tyrant, mustering small armies of people to do things. Merlin disliked him. He wouldn't turn on with 'the boys.' Mat Katz got into his pocketbook a couple of times and Graham was fence-sitting. He was never Sol Hurok or Norman Granz . . . he was Bill Graham with his own private vision and this much he deserves, he has individuated. But his noncommittal interface with the big hip community and his obviously uptown connections frightened a lot of people. Musicians by nature frighten easily and fall prey to all sorts of gossip. To counteract this paranoia and to provide an alternative to high prices and bad vibes, the Dead, the Airplane, and Quicksilver got together to open their own 'ballroom,' the old Carousel ballroom on Market Street. But it was a bummer from the beginning. One manager, Ron Rackow, fucked up a lot and Danny Rifkin ran off and the Carousel ran the shows their own way. People flooded in, but the bad vibes got no better.

Finally, Bill Graham co-opted this wayward musicians' commune and acquired the (Carousel) Fillmore West by flying to Ireland to sign a lease with the owner, something Rackow never thought to do. Howard Johnson is not putting up a hotel, so the era has ended – that part of the era, anyway. Besides, Merlin could never get the PA to work right. It was wired together with cynicism.

Tiff Garcia recalls one evening when he was standing next to Neal Cassady and swears he saw Neal levitate a 30-pound magnetic horn tweeter that was about to fall on some stoned girl in the front row. That was the Carousel way – salvation through psychokinesis.

By late 1967 the Carousel conglomerate idea was foundering from too much dream pipe and not enough decision making; that's what kills us all eventually.

Maybe the Carousel failure was more specifically due to the homogeneity of the bands; they all came from the same Stock Pot, the same Bay Area music scene. To some observers it was apparent that they were only 'brothers' to public view. Then, too, the who-gets-the-money question came up more than once, and the career stuff and the ego trips, and then there's the business of poor form in the dope room. In other words, some of the bands were doing heroin, while others strictly forbade it. Anyone with a wink of sense could figure out who the smack freaks were, most of 'em were dead already. After all, death is nature's way of warning us.

The Dead spearheaded the Carousel fantasy, Merlin put up his sound system and the Dead actually financed much of the loss. The demise of the Carousel ended in gloom for everyone, and the morale within the Grateful Dead establishment was at a peculiarly morbid low.

It was about this time that Phil freaked out on Wagner's Parsifalian idea of the invisible orchestra:

> How I detest this business of costumes and make-up, after creating the invisible orchestra I should like to invent the invisible theater as well . . .
>
> – Cosima's Diary 1878

I suppose this flash is a logical extension of the frustration of having to deal with instruments and stages and audiences and all these other layers of crap. Phil, like Wagner and Harry Haller and thousands of others, wanted to break through to a more direct mode of expression. Wouldn't a sub-vocal mind tap that could play directly into a tape be cleaner and nicer?

Well, Garcia finally got pissed off at that one.

We're gonna stick together and nobody's gonna cop out!

Garcia and Phil finally saw eye to eye to eye.

For the final Carousel gig, the combined groups decided to have a kind of acid test. A real blow-out, with everybody invited and no external publicity. The old Irish Tango Fox

Trot Parlor just wasn't the same after that. There were placards backstage that read: TANGO or CHA-CHA-CHA or RUMBA. Paul Foster, dressed in a set of coveralls and wearing his importancy hat, top hat with two white wings attached, inserted one of those dance cards so that everybody could see and it read simply:

FREAK FREELY

We did, they did, he she, it did, and after that night the Airplane and the Dead and Big Brother, with Janis and Quicksilver and the others, all went back to the insanity of their own private Karma.

Bill Graham was partially correct in assuming that he salvaged the San Francisco sound from the debris of the acid tests, but he didn't do it single-handedly. There were other businessmen around. People like John McIntyre from the Dead and Ron Polte of the Messenger Service helped this musical phoenix rise for one more giant toke. One more macrocosmic life breath pumped into this final horde, this final mixed bag of Druids and Thuggees, all trying to cop a feel of an ultimate reality that may or may not exist.

John McIntyre lights up like a sun for an instant, then dies down to normal. When he stands against a window the sun can reflect through him. You can see his veins under the skin, but it's not anemic. McIntyre is a purely Gothic creature. His brow resembles a Norseman's, but his facial features remind us of a debauched Hapsburg Count, gaunt and lean, long flowing mane of hair, most theatrical in itself – a Moslem with a Scotch last name – that's McIntyre.

He was fumbling with a bottle of cheap wine, hoping to get enough money together for a good bottle of Pouilly-Fuissé '38, when he met Danny Rifkin in LA. Rifkin was raving about his rock group, and John happened by to see what gives. Then later moved to the City to see 710 Ashbury.

After the Carousel, Mickey Hart's father, Lenny, stumbled in and borrowed money from everybody and split with a rather large SOME, and the lawyers took their share, and so went off the heat, and to cool out busts in New Orleans and the musicians wanted some, and dope costs a little, so the boys were always broke – the bills always behind

About 1969, McIntyre started managing the Grateful Dead. He was viper and head manager, then moved up to Grand Kleegle, and finally to Supreme Guardian of Angelic Mastery. I remember when I first met him he was hoping to acquire a rare Islamic manuscript (along with the wine, I guess) called the Necromicon of Abdul Hazred. This text is very powerful, and it is said to empower the reader of Allah with miraculous abilities, while cursing the eyes of the ignorant infidel who dares to breech its mysteries.

By 1971, the Dead got out of debt. David and Bonnie Parker came up from Palo Alto to manage the office and John worked the public relations scams.

Come hear Uncle John's band playing
to the tide.

Got some things to talk about here
beside the riverside . . .

But sometimes he gets nervous and disappears.

It was
McIntyre
who got the Dead to Europe, finally
(five years after the Jefferson Airplane).
Now
it's
the
Dead's
turn.

That's correct, you heard it right:

The Grateful Dead finally played the continent of Europe – France, to be exact. Hardly anybody heard about it . . . it wasn't really a gig. Originally it was to be a festival, but the arrival of the Dead was fraught with a myriad of small problems and infinite improbabilities.

The first and major improbability was the odd and curious truth that the festival was rained out . . . not a drizzle but a huge, torrential, howling downpour. This may not seem improbable until we realize that there hasn't been a rainstorm of that proportion in June in France for about a century.

The second improbability was that a Frenchman would send the Dead enough money to ship up and get it on. All the crew, the Alembic sound technicians, Merlin's famous de-bugged PA, a translator, a photographer, the managers and about half the family came along. All this because a guy named Jean Bouquin was throwing a big party. Bouquin himself is an improbability, and his improbabilities probably cancel out some of the others. He's a high-fashion dress designer, with customers like Madame Onassis and B.B.; yet he's no fop or dandy: He shaves occasionlly, wears loafers with no sox, wears long antique scarves over Montgomery-Ward's crew-neck sweaters, with no undershirt . . . he's Lenny Bruce's definition of a tough guy . . . yet he's a millionaire. He decided to throw a festival to break up the ennui at his very posh and notorious boutique near St Germain.

The third improbability was that the festival was to be held on a western-style dude ranch near Auvers, a bright little village about forty kilometers northeast of Paris. The signs on the dude ranch just about blew everybody's mind. We came from Marin County, which is a dude ranch of sorts, and we find ourselves confronted with a sign that reads:

Auvers in Texas, Texas in Auvers Dude Ranch

Now, it seems a bit incongruous to run across this little location in the midst of what some of the entourage thought was a Gallic enlightenment. The buildings were like stage sets from Paramount's back lot: quick wooden buildings, with no plumbing except the usual Gallo-Roman latrine.

Immediately adjacent to this site – the dude ranch took up about forty acres – was a little white farmhouse belonging to the Comtesse Vavin, who was coughing loudly and calling the National Guard, with their little blue official hats and praying for rain. Bouquin forgot to tell her that her little scene was being overrun by a bunch of wild hares trampling on her wheatfields, and that the stage was forty yards from her cottage.

The publicity was bad, too. In no time the word got out that a festival was being held – and although the Dead were being assured that it was cool, it was in fact very uncool to announce a FREE FESTIVAL. 'FREE FREEDOM THREE DAYS' was what the arrows pointed toward . . . in green day glo ink. Now there's a curious thing happens when ya throw a free festival: The people think it's free to get in, if they can get in, but two million English musicians think it means that anybody can come to jam . . . this was not specifically delineated in the publicity prior to the concern, so about forty down-and-out groups put all their equipment into their ubiquitous Thames lorries and drove to Dover to catch the boat train.

Another improbable event took place after the rain-out. The Dead were supposed to stay at a chateau near the festival grounds, and a chateau it was . . . it turns out Bouquin has a deal cookin' with a well-known French composer and film-score writer named Michel Magne. Using his fame, he managed to grab onto an abandoned Louis-the-14th Chateau near Auvers . . . see what I mean . . . thick as thieves, in an even weirder small village called Herouville. The chateau was almost burned down after the French Revolution and stood full of cows for almost a hundred years. After World War II, Magne managed to convince the government that he should buy the property and tear down the chateau and build a spa resort on the site; for this he got a fantastic tax break [possession is ten points of the law]. He then turned to restoring the place to health that would have made Louix XIV slobber. Namely, he installed wiring, a tennis court, a large outdoor pool and guess what? . . . a huge recording studio. That's right, the whole festival was put together to get the Dead and some other groups to be aware of the recording studio and health spa.

Unlike U.S. studios' rates, Strawberry Studios, as the

place is called, includes room and Baronial board in the prix fixe. The Dead flashed on it as a good place to do a runaway album. But there's another aspect to it: The good vibes of an inn in the storm gave way to an ominous presence . . . almost like it could be a prison . . . there was even a rook and dungeon dated 1841 hidden in the back garden.

On Saturday night, the storm got worse. In spite of the fistfights on the dude ranch, the castle was quiet; Pig Pen drank some unmarked branch water and got the French Ague, and Garcia crashed for twenty-four hours. As the hysteria mounted, a rumor circulated that someone was beaten up in Paris . . . some rival promoter. The boys had never been to Paris . . . and the people that met us at the airport refused to drive through Paris to get us to the chateau, taking a weird, meandering and circuitous course around the city . . . almost as if we were chattel to someone's serfdom . . . which, as it turned out, we were. Now John McIntyre was sharp! He got us there with no commitments, no paper contract; if they didn't like the scene the boys wouldn't play . . . 'No more Altamonts' is the byword these days. However, there was a very neat contract between Michel Magne and Jean Bouquin to cover recording of the festival and housing the various artists that were supposed to show up. The Shanana were actually stuck in Heathrow, London, for eight hours and had to go right back to New York. Can you see that mad scene: The Dead and the Shanana living out a French rainstorm in a haunted castle where Chopin used to woodshed, and where Jean Cocteau actually wrote 'Blood of a Poet'? That's another one of those improbabilities.

On Sunday the weather was still ominous and the plot thickened. Pig Pen was still comatose, but Garcia and Phil wanted to play music . . . no one wanted to see Paris right away. Florence Nathan was born in Paris and spoke fluid French; Ron Rackow, the perennial geography scout, was there in 1970 for about a month; but the rest of the people were sort of crapped out and scared. Still, somehow they arranged to take three separate junkets in a rented Mercedes-Benz. The first trip consisted of Bob Weir, Bill

Kreutzmann, and finally, Garcia, the driver and Florence. The second wave took Bob Hunter and Bonnie Parker, the office manageress, and two people from the Alembic crew. Ram Rod and Jackson never did get into Paris, and Pig Pen never knew he was in France.

The tour route was simple . . . all sights of Paris at 60 KM per hour takes two hours . . . if you blink fast enough it can be memorized like a big stroboscopic blur for future reference. First Etoile and the Arc de Triomphe. Weir wanted to know if anybody knew who the Unknown Soldier really was. Then Tour Eiffel . . . second-stage only. While there, some long-haired American ran up to Garcia and said, 'Jesus Christ, Jerry Garcia, what'r you doin' here?' This unction was aided by a big pat on the back that makes Garcia nervous; humble Garcia simply hunches his shoulders and says: 'Oh jeez, seein' the sights!' . . . all the while considering a number of more cynical remarks.

Next, a very quick pace through the Champs Elysées; then a right just before the Place de la Concorde, and down under the bridges on the River Gauche, and surface at Notre Dame . . . catch a quick tourist coffee, then out of town through Montparnasse . . . follow the signs to Pontoise . . . that's it . . . rock and roll view of Paris . . . but we'll be back for sure, we all said.

On Monday the sky cleared to a glorious impressionist canvas: Monet lily pad, trees, and the last Seurat dots. Some people sat up all night by the fire on Ritalin and realized it can all be done without acid if there is a sun that rises at four a.m. and birds that clear their throats in gnarled pepper trees, and lots of French girls that our gracious host made to appear and disappear at proportionate intervals . . . all of it saying: 'Come back . . . imprisonment here won't be so bad . . . we only want some money from Warner Brothers!'

John McIntyre was nowhere to be found, hiding in Paris at a friend's house. The guy who answered the phone had instructions to deny John's existence to anyone who should call . . . John was right in the middle of all of the intrigues and he had to bury his lion-maned head for awhile.

Still the last Monday in June was glorious! Mars was

uare to Jupiter, and Jupiter stood affixed to the old church steeple in Herouville exactly at sunrise on the Summer Solstice . . . the church steeple marked with the sign of the Ram, and the clock stopped at 6:32, 1944, never to be unrusted . . . all of the portents were obvious: it was a weird time.

At about lunch on Monday, Michel had laid out his usual chateau luncheon consisting of cold cuts, peaches and fruit, french bread, house wine and coffee . . . it was over this feast that Phil and Jerry decided to play outside that night . . . assuming the weather held. Everybody went into a frenzy. I drove to Paris to get my friend André Bercoff of 'L'Express.' 'Paris Match' found out about it . . . the Grateful Dead would play live, free, outdoors, for the townspeople of Herouville, and the press and anybody else. About two hundred people finally showed up . . . it was a grande fête for Michel and Bouquin, and it was a diplomatic and fitting climax to a brief sojourn in France, like a touchdown in an ongoing game.

By three o'clock the equipment was set up, the bright tie-dyes that had never been seen in Europe before, the California tribal banners stretched out in peaceful array, the three tons of mechaniques finally out of the truck and on display. The French electronics nuts went wild . . . the press went wild . . . the local peasants drank themselves into oblivion . . . the baron had finally opened up the wine cellar for them and they got shit-face drunk.

The Dead started to play just before the sky got dark, but their entire set was illuminated by bright lights from the Paris socialized television station LINK TWO, which rebroadcast the event the next week. Their film technique was flawless, as one would expect from a French film team; the camera people were completely unobtrusive on the musicians; the lights bugged Phil a little. Pig Pen just barely recovered in time to sing after downing his two bottles of duty-free Wild Turkey . . . Weir was in fine primal scream voice, and Garcia settled into his trancelike lassitude from which emanates the famous electronic genius that is particularly his.

They played for three hours, and during this time the

workers and the fire department and little children lit hundreds of candles and placed them around the pool as if it were a religious shrine . . . a Lourdes or place of healing waters. As the party progressed, the candles were extinguished by the bodies of various drunken celebrants being thrown in the pool by other drunken celebrants. The Dead played louder and louder; the locals never heard anything like it before and they were delirious.

Throughout this entire event, Bill Ham and his light show people and the musicians from the *LIGHT SOUND DIMENSION BAND* were waiting to play. Finally, the Dead got exhausted. The *LSD BAND* played next and the light show flared up. It was marvelous . . . they played in the dark (like the old days) but like professionals. The musicians stood or sat facing the light-show screen on the other side of the grounds, about 30 meters away. First time I had ever seen a light show played to musicians directly and musicians watching the light show feed back on them. The lead singer with the group had a marvelous witch voice, piercing the dark and sending everyone into a trance of recollection for the days of inner trips. We had all heard it before; it was like planet music, but not quite this planet: it was as if some other planet-people had studied Earth music and then gone back to integrate it into their own forms. The early morning had become unearthly cold, made everything grind to a halt.

Lesh finally got into Paris, because I begged him to go along, as I had to take some people back and it was 3:00 in the morning . . . I might fall asleep at the wheel. We saw the sun rise on Notre Dame on the solstice . . . then we split. The plane left for San Francisco around noon the same day, and it was over for the musicians as suddenly as it began.

I stayed another week, traveled to Amsterdam and saw Pink Floyd get rained out, too. But there were no fistfights, no Americans; just 60,000 Dutch bicycle-riding freaks. The American tourists were all down at the Dam Square, trying to score some hash and talking to other Americans, completely oblivious to the free Sunday concert in the park. Amsterdam is a fine place to live if one can forget about

America for a few minutes. Why not? The Dutch do it all the time! You see, America just ain't very important sometimes.

The street is rainy but Amsterdam is quiet, and it's Saturday night, and I was sold a membership to the Club Paradiso, and I spent about twenty minutes in there and it blew me out. It looks like a scene from a Warhol movie, but with more people. Everybody, I mean everybody, on the nod . . . not high . . . on the nod. No speed or acid around, but so much hash you wouldn't believe it. Bought some medium-grade Kief for about 20 guilders, which is $5.40 American (and that was for four grams) and went out on the verandah to dig the light show. It was a copy of a bad, early makeshift show. Listened to a group of freaks from one of the Dutch colonies playing through a bad Telefunken PA. And I sez to myself, 'Ya' know, the Dead may never play Amsterdam, and if they don't play Amsterdam they won't really ever play Europe except via the small little Wurlitzer-Phillips-Norelco-Quaker-Oats boxes that most Amsterdamers play music on. It's amazing how they can hear those things at all and call it fidelity, but they do, and they scream for the Dead. But the Dead ain't gonna show up till the PA is right, and until the one-time promoters (everywhere) come down off their greed trips and get it to the people straight.

In the meantime, the Continent sleeps through interminable chains of flagellating rock groups and soul singers and acid rockettes that seem to play Europe because they were doing a gig in England, anyway, so they get booked into three nights in Berlin and the Germans wonder what the hell that is. 'It is the San Francisco sound, Herr Schneble?'

I'm standing on this balcony in Paradiso, which was the church, and the Bill Graham of Amsterdam pushed me off the back end because I'm disturbing the maestro, who's doing his light show number, and I take one last long look over the side and see the freaks (who are not sitting attentively but who are, instead, comatose). I leave, escorted by the truly most far-out person in Amsterdam, Simon Vinkenoog, the Dutch writer who has yet to be really big in the States except for his exquisite anthology, *The Book of*

Grass (Grove Press), but who has published 27 books and is so famous here that the cabdrivers know where he lives.

Simon seems jaded, or at least oblivious to the sea of bodies that I'm walking through. It's one big, giant crash-pad, and the Club Paradiso is more like Purgatorio – worse than the Haight-Ashbury Clinic at full-tilt summer of '67. But it dawns on me that the Dutch heat is much hipper than the American heat, because Amsterdam is peppered with hostels where one can indulge to his heart's content, and ya' know what? Ya' can leave your house unlocked in Amsterdam and your car unattended, and ya' won't get burned because the keeds are in Paradiso and Fantasio getting high and staying high, and it turns out that this was the idea of the Provos back in '65. The government went for it, and it works. Most of these places were churches at one time, except one which was a huge milk-processing plant, and it appears that going to one of these dormitory hash dens is the thing to do if you're 18 in Amsterdam. The Paradiso was jammed, poorly ventilated and poorly decorated (or should I say vandalized?). But still, the Dutch and the American tourists queue up for blocks to get in, just as they did for 'Woodstock.'

The genius that gave us Rembrandt van Rijn needs a shot in the ass, and the Zeitgeist that gave the world Seurat is being acted upon by an external force and needs a hotmeat injection. The free music has the power to call down the dynes of magnetic energy that stretch along the dragon paths of Europe. If this happens, there will be a serious and rapid ex-patriot movement. For the time being, however, home will have to do.

I'm sitting in Vinkenoog's office in Amsterdam, with the world globe lit up, and remembering Phil and me discussing Stonehenge just before I split for Europe. And we thought it might be a good idea to have a new focus fantasy one that would solidify the family, one that would bring the world together (if possible), and we discussed the idea of playing certain ancient music on top of Silbury Hill (St Michael's Hill) near Glastonbury because it is nature's ultimate wonderful amphitheater, with seating for three billion in the wage of the Dragon in the path of the pilgrims who came in other times. This would be the ultimate gathering, contrary to Woodstock, the Umveldt shared by all. And we discussed having representatives from every 'head' family get together and form 'charter affinity-infinity groups' to fly to Silbury to revere each other as was done in Megalithic times on that spot and for no bread – for no money at all, for nothing whatever except worship of the divine geometry.

I spent the Fourth of July watching a Mao-Tse-Tung documentary on Dutch TV and listening to a British radio station in Switzerland broadcast fairly wide-spectrum rock, with no commercials. That station, however, is being jammed by Radio Free Europe, Dutch Radio, and BBC, alternatively. First the BBC jam comes in – a long binodal warble; then the pirate station tunes that out and we hear five clear minutes of Aretha singing 'Soul Man'; then BEEP . . . BEEP, the Dutch found the frequency and put their little obnoxious jammer into gear. That drowned out the Scotch weather report and about three verses of 'Johnny-B-Good.' Then wam-wam-wam, in comes Chuck Berry very loud, so I had to turn down the radio, and then finally turned it off when Radio Free Europe put on the static and gave a little plug for the Army Translation Corps at Badabling Station, outside Munich. I said, 'Ah, shit!' Maybe the Commies would be better.

But then I realized the Grateful Dead will probably never play Leningrad, either (as revolutionary as they are), because an established régime hates anything beautiful, 'specially music that frees the soul in some way.

All I know for certain is that the Americans don't have a thing on the Europeans in general. Maybe the plumbing is better in California, but the food in Switzerland is mostly organic. You can smell it in the morning. Maybe we've got more TV, but in Europe TV ain't the big God's Eye it is at home, and commercials are despised in most cases.

The important thing we have in common is music. It's too much to be stuck in a French traffic jam in the Place de la Concorde on Bastille Day and be listening to Guitar Slim singing 'Down Home Girl.' It's too much to be speeding around roads in Switzerland and hear Dylan comin' through with 'Early Morning Rain.' Ah, who gives a shit, anyway! It's all free.

The ideal of the free gig, the 'turn-you-on-gig-for-free,' started with the Dead and will continue with the Dead. And like the 'free music,' the people should be free, and so should medicine, and dental care, and psychotherapy. Who cares if the Grateful Dead are the Thelonius Monk of Europe? But let's examine why Thelonius never shows up: Integrity, that's what it's all about – that's the key to the whole drop-out ethic. The Dead are still together because they work hard – harder than anybody I've ever seen. That's why 'Workingman's Dead' was so popular. And they work at things the public never sees.

How about Jerry working onstage all night with his ensembles and practicing about four hours a day and recording twenty hours a week? These cats put in a seventy-hour week of work, and they get energy from nowhere. They've consumed at least five managers and truckloads of equipment over the years.

And that's the message in the music, too. Work yer ass off . . . there ain't nothin' else to do but dream and work, and work some more. It don't matter none where life is at; we all know the universe is absurd, but why sit and wait for the Zen tiger to snap your head off?

Now, you have met some of the entelechies that have advanced the San Francisco underground one quantum jump further. Garcia will always be a virtuoso; he plays music every day, gets nervous when he can't be around his instruments, and is perpetually working. He did the sound track for an Antonioni movie, *Zabriskie Point*, plays pedal steel guitar for THE NEW RIDERS OF THE PURPLE SAGE, and will undoubtedly be playing until he joyfully drops from exhaustion.

Phil is headed toward the great electronic future with more advanced compositions in mind. He works now on computer designs and new music for the Twenty-First Century. But his daily Grateful Dead dose is good medicine. Tom Constantin dropped out from the drop-outs into Scientology, and he's now designing a rock opera based on Frankenstein. Mickey Hart has his own studio in the woods,

Pig Pen will always sing blues, and Weir is tomorrow's super-star, but everybody in the band will always be into music.

The point is that it ain't gonna end so soon. The Grateful Dead will be singin' and pickin' for a long era to come, and the family will probably always be cohesive. The family, you see, is a model for other families seeking alternative life styles.

So what I'm sayin' is that the Grateful Dead family is finally together. Neal Cassady used to say, 'If ya' wanna live high, ya' gotta get high,' and that is what has happened. Old swords are cased; noses are counted. Garcia steps up in front and makes a perfect gesture akin to a Mudra (but with a little Outer Mission thrown in) which instantly flashes a feeling of well-being.

In other words, some of the poverty paranoia of the Haight period, circa 1965, is being, or has been, expunged. The Dead can all read music fluently and write it, and they can all teach each other to a high degree of communication, which in the early days was what took so long. Jerry tirelessly gave away all his used-up secret riffs and went to the bottom of the well and found an infinity of new stuff.

It seems eerie to see Garcia pulling away into the foggy Marina streets in a '48 Bentley . . . after the Corvair and the Bus, but there he goes. WHOOSH! No rattles, no hood ornament, sculptured fenders. Concours d'élégance. Trying to blow David Crosby's mind, trying to slip a wink at Phil now and again, onstage; and from everywhere, the spies stretch out. The family is a business now, but what has it to show
for its
giant, aching,
absurd
waste of
TIME?

Merlin made dope for everybody. That's a fact! The Boys made Street Music and the equipment got up on time (sometimes) and the modern idiom was wrenched asunder! The free music is here! Maybe under a different name, but it's here.

But more than music, that uncompromising integrity is

here, refreshing in the junkpile of souls. To give hope to the future, Neal once told Odduck: 'Never trust a man who doesn't have kids!'

The Planet Earth Rock and Roll Orchestra is upon us. To quote Stockhausen, 'Musicians who practice the TRADE of music today, the dominant older men, are acting out an automatic unconscious lack of enthusiasm.'

The music of the 1970s, the big free sound, is the music of the entirety of future generations; it is the fundamental music sometimes disguised as blues, sometimes a hoard of serene power, creating higher levels of awareness that are frightening to some, as they do not wish to see a higher level of awareness, or anything other than the ego state that most poisons them.

Thus, these people do not evolve. They stay behind as dogs in caverns, looking with contempt as the new visionary tribes move on to the bright meadows of the future.

The free music is the Grateful Dead and their pals, and they are only the second beginning. Neolithic music was also free; that's what this is – an enlightenment of magick, not a renaissance, as some would have us believe, but a return to Stone Age magick – and there are those even more profound to follow . . . through this gateless gate.